DAUGHTER ISOTOPE

vidhu aggarwal

the operating system's unlimited editions
print//document

DAUGHTER ISOTOPE

ISBN: 978-1-946031-90-7
Library of Congress Catalogue-in-Publication Number: 2021941578
copyright © 2021 by Vidhu Aggarwal
interior design by Vidhu Aggarwal with the OS Open Design Protocol
cover design by Elæ Moss

As of 2020 all titles are available for donation-only download via our Open Access Library:
www.theoperatingsystem.org/os-open-access-community-publications-library/

The Operating System is a member of the **Radical Open Access Collective**, a community of scholar-led, not-for-profit presses, journals and other open access projects. Now consisting of 40 members, we promote a progressive vision for open publishing in the humanities and social sciences. *Learn more at:* http://radicaloa.disruptivemedia.org.uk/about/

Typography: This text was set in Commune Nuit Debout, Freight, PT Sans Narrow, Minion, OCR-A Standard, Futura, Baskerville, Tahoma, Impact, Helvetica Neue, and Budmo Jiggler. Commune, our title font, is used via a SIL Open Font License, through Velvetyne Type Foundry. It was designed by Sébastian Marchal. All type on VTF is libre and open-source, and fully aligned with the OS's mission. Support their work and learn more at https://velvetyne.fr

About the cover: a new digital rendering by Elæ Moss of a film still from 'Manifest Humpadori,' shot by Nilu Amin, envisioned by Aggarwal as "cosmic bride" and/or a vision of the Ardhanarishvara Shiva, inhabiting both male and female forms.

Your donation makes our publications, platform and programs possible! We <3 You.
http://theoperatingsystem.org/subscribe-join/

the operating system

www.theoperatingsystem.org
operator@theoperatingsystem.org
IG: @the_operating_system
tweettweet: @the_os_

DAUGHTER ISOTOPE

For Vijay Kumar Aggarwal

 *"Enter a cloud
And things are blotted out, ruins restored"*

– *Meena Alexander, from "Aesthetic Knowledge"*

DAUGHTER ISOTOPE

In nuclear physics, an unstable nuclei or isotope of an element (such as uranium-238) spontaneously decays to another isotope — a *daughter* — with an attendant release of energy.

"Some isotopes decay and immediately produce a stable daughter product...Others decay and produce unstable daughters, which then become the parent products of their own daughters. Unstable isotopes producing unstable daughters form a *radioactive decay chain*.

Using empirical data, it is possible to statistically forecast what percentage of a radioisotope's population will decay over a given period of time. This has enabled workers to define a *half-life* for each radioisotope, the period required for one-half of the original parent population to decay to its daughter product.

Through time, the number of parents constantly decreases while the number of daughters constantly increases. Theoretically, although the number of parents will become insignificantly small, there should never come a time when all of the parent population has decayed to daughters.

Knowing the value of a specific isotope's half-life, it is possible to determine the age of a geologic or archaeologic sample by evaluating the amount of parent and daughter isotopes in it."

Steven L. Goldstein and Sidney Hemming,
"Isotopes and Radioactivity Tutorial"

Nature is a temple of living columns,
Where words often come out in in haze.
Man wanders in these forests of symbols:
They observe him with a knowing gaze.

– Charles Baudelaire, from "Correspondances"

"I do not know just what it is that I am like. I wander about concealed and wrapped in thought."

– The Rig Veda (1.164.37), translated by Wendy Doniger

"I wandered lonely as a a cloud"

– William Wordsworth

A cloud, as a permeable, networked digital archive, a *deus ex machina*, or the search engine for the lyric poem: "I wandered lonely as a cloud"

 American fast food a la the hamburger (centered on a patty composed of beef, prohibited in Hinduism)

 In the Mahabharata, Sanskrit epic of war, archery is the definitive military skill, mastered by Arjun, a prince known as the "greatest" warrior of his age, despite rivals with equal or greater skill

 Panchajanya conch, war horn of Krishna, an avatar of Vishnu, Hindu god of preservation and renewal, and the best friend of Arjun

 Padma Vyuha or Lotus Formation, a deadly maze-like military formation in the 18-day war described in the Mahabharata; or any bewildering system, conundrum, or daunting, inaccessible plane

 A whirligig, a revolving door, or a gyrating weather system, such as a cyclone or tornado, that serves as a portal or portent

 Flying Kali yantra, a geometric shape representing the entropic and regenerative facets of the Hindu goddess, or Devi (Draupadi, the "Helen of Troy" of the epic Mahabharata, is, at times, viewed as an avatar of Devi in this aspect)

 Harappan seal of a mysterious, horned, hoofed meditating figure from the Indus Valley civilization, called a proto-Shiva, after the god of primal energies and beasts; a chimera (see minotaur)

 Shiva-linga, pharmaceutical capsule, cannister, or other site of contained energies

 Domestic dog from a Roman mosaic found at Pompei; a stray dog follows King Yudhisthira (Arjun's brother), in his final, arduous jouney to swarga (heaven), where dogs are generally excluded; dharma of the aspirant, the follower, the "minor" character

 Harappan seal depicting either domestic cattle, or the earliest known image of the unicorn

 The dice game of the gods initiate the four ages (yugas) in the Vedic cycle of time with increasing entropy as the ages progress (a pivotal dice game in the Mahabharata during the third age leads to an apocalyptic war)

 Radioactive isotope, unstable contanminated material, or nuclear hazard, housed in Rutherford's now defunct model of the atom, which nevertheless demonstrates that matter is mostly composed of empty space

 Biohazard, a common sign in the Kali Yuga, the last of four ages of increasing disorder in the the Vedic cycle of time

 Angel of hazards, Angel in the House, or other prophetic, networked, engineered server

 A detached head, via the portrait of poet E. Dickinson as a teenager, which she reportedly did not like, but which has been fetishized ad nauseum since her death; the head mostly disappears, except for the collar, indicating an individualized A.I. unit

 An aspirational site, akin to an imaginary homeland, channeling feminine cosmic energies

 A spectral site, body, or filter (see famous song "Somewhere Over the Rainbow," from *The Wizard of Oz*, a film in which a rainbow never appears)

 Vishnu's command via Sudarshana Chakra, his serrated disk of "auspicious vision," sometimes activated as a weapon or discoball; Vishnu's navel out of which a lotus blooms; or detector of known and unknown fundamental particles and energies

 Vehicle for traveling between material and virtual planes; Venus (Roman love goddes), Saraswati Devi (Hindu goddess of knowledge associated with pooling waters and rivers), and Manasa Devi, (goddess of snakes, associated with forests), all ride on swan mounts

"Whatever is here about dharma, profit, pleasure, and release is also found elsewhere, but what is not here is found nowhere else..."
— The Mahabharata (18.5.38), translated by Wendy Doniger

VYASA CLOUD

Vyasa was born in a cloud and hence was and is a cloud. Vyasa is a cloud full of semen, and hence a father. Vyasa became a father so he could be a cloud. Vyasa's father was also a cloud who was a rishi with the magical power of conjuring up clouds. Vyasa's father slept with a girl on a boat and shielded his antics from her stern father with cloud. The girl was a fishergirl. Before she entered the cloud, she smelled like fish. After she entered the cloud, she smelled like celestial petals. The cloud also restored her virginity along with giving her a magnificent seductive scent like no other woman, so one day she would become a queen. Hence, Vyasa's father the rishi was both a cloud and a perfumery and a conveyor of royalty. Vyasa's mother paddled her boat into the cloud with the rishi and had an instant child before anyone noticed and his name was Vyasa. The cloud was like an egg. Out of it hatched a grown man, Vyasa. How could a young girl give birth to a grown man unless she birthed a cloud? Because Vyasa was a cloud at birth, he could go away and immediately do the work of a scholar and archivist, studying and compiling the Vedas; he could write books that someone else—an elephant-headed god, for instance—would transcribe; write books like the Mahabharata, the epic chronicle where he told the story of his birth as cloud. Vyasa told his mother, the fishergirl, that he would return whenever she called for him even though he would be busy studying, archiving, and writing books because a cloud can come and go.

Vyasa was by all accounts, especially his own—an indifferent father. A cloud is a father who comes and goes, who comes and goes for centuries and generations, like Vyasa. When his mother finally called for him, after she had married a great king and had others kids, who had all died unexpectedly, Vyasa appeared before her like a dirty unkempt cloud. At his mother's bequest, Vyasa interrupted his bookish meditations, and sired several kids with the widowed princesses of the rightful heirs of the Kuru clan, Vyasa's dead younger brothers. Therefore, it was put upon Vyasa to perpetuate the royal lineage, even though he himself was an unkempt rishi and not royal, not descended from Bharata or Shantanu, but a cloud. He frightened the widowed princesses with his unkempt vaporousness. They closed their eyes or turned pale at his vaporous approach so Vyasa cursed their offspring, his own sons, the heirs of empire, to be unprepared for the job. He cursed one son to be blind, both in the regular fashion and morally. He cursed his other son to be sickly, sick at heart and soul. He cursed his own sons so that he could have a story to tell about kingship, about the vagaries of inheritance. The entire royal lineage was under dispute, under a cloud, because of Vyasa. Vyasa wrote about his kids, and his kids' kids, and his kids' kids' kids and the bloody war they fought about their claims to Bharat, a great empire. He wrote about how his kids and his kids' kids and his kids' kids' kids were mutilated or decapitated or heartbroken by this dispute. At every turn, Vyasa would come and go and make sure the war would happen, so he could write about it. Maybe in order to write about a war you must be disembodied from your own kin, you must be a cloud. Even though Vyasa knew one set of his grandkids would be evil and obnoxious, he magically appeared to assist in their mutant births so that eventually they would start a war with his other set of noble grandkids. Vyasa split the hard ball of a mutant embryo which his daughter-in-law—the blindfolded queen of his blind son—beat out of her own body. He split this hard ball into one hundred evil sons with a bit leftover for a girl. While each one of these hundred sons perished in the war in Kurukshetra, it isn't clear what happened to the daughter.

But it's certain, Vyasa was born in a cloud and hence was and is a cloud. Sometime a cloud can be big and sometimes a cloud can be small. Sometimes a cloud can split into other clouds like celestial petals, and float here and there. Some as big as the globe, some as small as insects. Many fathers were clouds, many mothers were clouds, and they would come and go. Many of these many clouds went to Africa or the Caribbean or Europe. Some of these clouds went to the United States of America. These clouds followed many people around, entering and exiting quickly or slowly. Once a young girl entered into a cloud and while there, she ordered a hamburger. A hamburger and French fries. This particular cloud, which was one of many, had not heard hamburger and French fries spoken before with such ebullience and ease. Because this cloud, like every other cloud, had everything in it of profit, pleasure and dharma, it now had hamburgers too, and French fries. Hamburger and French fries, pronounced with such glee, so that the cloud too was delighted. The cloud spoke freely to the girl and said I want more hamburger and French fries. The cloud said I am your father Vyasa and you are Vyasa too, and you have the blessings of the magical word hamburger. You have the blessings of American English, not that hoity-toity *English* English that broke me, but another English—even more greedy—that loves guns and fast food. Openly, openly! And I would like to order some global English with those hamburgers and fries. And celestial petals or clouds cascaded all over the girl. But she brushed them off and moved on. She brushed them off without a care for anything but hamburgers and French fries and magazines and video games and late nite TV, while the world melted and burned. But the girl didn't know that every time she ordered hamburgers or fries she was eating celestial petals. She was eating clouds. The girl didn't know that after entering into that cloud, she was forever smelling of grease and ketchup, a wafting aroma. Even though clouds come and go, and go and go, spawning more clouds, everywhere more, the girl didn't know that she was already a cloud, disembodied from her kin. That one day she would grow up to be a cloud, that she was always a cloud, who would come and go, go and go.

Father holds up a cloud, a glowing, seething archive, vibrating with code, a book with everything in it, and says beti: from this, you will translate our history.

There is another me in a parallel universe lunging in warrior asana, with the time and discipline to attend to the flitting syntax of clouds, telling me to "go girl."

There is yet another me in a parallel universe, legs folded in lotus asana, balanced precariously on a cloud, immersed in the language of gurus, who spits on my efforts.

And yet another, crushed by market forces, head and torso twisted sideways at an impossible angle, whispering "go girl."

And still another, contorted in an identical position but in reverse—as if in mirror world, giving me permanent side-eye.

And then another, crouched in an obscene squat, who says the book of books is a pathological contrivance, goading me to embrace my animal life.

And yet another, who has ten arms, one of which holds up the severed head of the father, none of which holds a single book.

THE GOLDEN EMBRYO

"The seven half-embryos portion out the semen of the world at Vishnu's command."
— The Rig Veda (1.164.36), *translated by Wendy Doniger*

Shiniest of voids, ringing with fields.
A unitary vigor, tarrying for eons.

Pluck the tension, and particles ding-dong and disappear.

Some clump and explode,
rainbow into uterine layers, diaphanous

and thickening—tabs

of bursting
cartographies.

Plasma membranes, oceanic feeling circulating
through straying habitats.

Life forms mutate, accumulating cultures. Some survive
the high waters, the freezes,

the anus of inverse allotments, abutting domains
of empire:

(. . . Araby shags Katharina, Prabu shanks birth,
Aaron ghosts haughty, Huck drags folks,
Bill tells stories, Julius sucks ore,
Vassily bots hard, Larry cracks jokes,
Darren bathes guns in power and glory. . .)

Lords of riches,
releasing remote intricate gizmos, repellents,
and horndog fantasies
into the loosening and baying expanses.

Who will embrace all

those odd, incidental creatures
ad infinitum,

as they are going, gone? One bug,
diamond-headed, inky,
with a cinched oblong body, pinched
at each end, with the slightest filament for a tail, and round,
sheer wings.

Lords of dissolution,
you will not be consoled: for being so torn

for missing always
the teeming void, the book of beginnings,

where you are decaying at every instant. At every instant,
anything goes: woozy pupae cluster upon splintering genealogies,

spitting out eccentric yantras with jazzy segments and alarming
high-pitched whines. Whatever's

left of that initial,

irradiated substrate

is on heightened alert, flashing skirts of squalor,

converting over—in and out of—time

into daughters.

THE BOOK OF BEGINNINGS

(Draupadi)

Sacrifice is a medium

for uncertain gains, a transactional
bubble full of fire and ghee and vital fluids.

Toss in some angry ejaculate, royal spunk,
and something extra materializes out of the flames.

At the flashpoint of a major yajna,
a wheeling pyramid of dairymaids straight out of the imaginary of priests.

One peels off the wheel into the real, alright!

Giddyup altar bleeding fire.
Augur a warrior, and out shoots a boy with a sword,

plus one
stunning daughter, caramelized, molting embers,
auguring the destruction of the entire warrior race.

 (I find myself in a transactional bubble floating in hilarity and commodities,
 twinned to entropy, and dripping with gems and brocades, alright!)

In the chemical chain reaction of a sacred fire, an exodus
through ever hotter hinges, masturbating

to free radicals,

a blissed out radioactive glow, endless desire suspended

above the known world,
then punctured by the straightest arrow, drawn by the finest warrior of his age—

(where I flop into an epic, slipformed and formalized, married to strangers)

and later, streams of arrows, catapults,

and celestial bombs, the floating kind,

the kind that effervesce before discharging

spherical attacks

against the present. Now just sink into the

past, you cannot help it.

Her voice, her livid scowls
possess you. Her combustive shadows

singeing you to the marrow
for centuries! Fire-born, Agni-jyotsna—she's really
that good, alright! A burning field, a conflagration.

Your insides jiggle up: offerings—
arias, incantations, mysterious bite marks. You cannot
help it.

You cannot help but swallow

the hallowed flames,
cradle the point, savor
the whistling arrow as you plummet into havoc and debris.

SWAMP OF VYASA

I clang my big
nose against the dank
relic and bob up. An ancient fuel tank?

Face caked
in chemical grit,
I spit out

minnows,
green-gold translucencies
with two tails. Mutant fish.

One try. One fail.
Once again, I must shed
my inhibitions. Once again, I dunk

my head, lobbing at the slimy
underwater bulk. No grip.
It hauls my body up instead:

a scalloped metal breastplate, brilliant—
the interior sludged
with blood

and nodules of torn skin, like suction cups
that work their way into
my chest. I puff out gold-red.

The armor gives my body heft.
Half-submerged in muck, I wait.
Maybe it is harder

to drown than I thought.
There's no time left
to steer myself toward another fate.

Bent to task, I guide
my heavy torso through the scum
of end-of-days, a thick paste

of effluents. No time really
to dawdle, complain.
I push my body through the pain,

down the shallows, beneath
the lily pads, where some
radioactive alligator must crave

my flesh. I trawl the bottom
and raise up sediment. Dark
on dark, so at first I don't

notice anything but my dark thoughts.
But something must be lighting
up the silt and fronds.

Not sun. Not jellyfish,
nor electric eel.
I see a thumb,

neon blue, almost transparent,
a gift of oxygen. I breathe it in, despite myself:
the thumb of Ekalavya, young

archer, never acclaimed
for his glorious flex and aim.
Dark, a forest dweller,

he was no prince.
But his mad skills
put a prince to shame. He could

make individual shoots of grass sting the air
and ring a moving target: muzzle
the booming growl

of the prince's hound
with an exquisite crown
of sharpened twigs, the dog

unhurt. He could catch
sound in its tracks. Scary good.
So they maimed him.

But the story went,
Ekalavya gave his thumb
away himself—cut his self-taught

genius to the quick. Stumped
and lost his hard-won knack
with shafts of any scale or kind

at the request of a great
guru who once rejected him
and wanted only a prince

to be the best. Tricked the boy
through his own deep reverence
for the great man's greatness.

A slash of honor—*gurudhakshina*—
that makes no sense
even here in the great, great murk—

where I lurch at any shaft of breath, where
I can barely   even
lose myself.

Draupadi, Draupadi, Draupadi, OOOOOOOhhhhhhh!

Draupadi, Draupadi, Draupadi, OOOOOOOhhhhhhh!

On one side an ovule, on one side a corpse,
a dhoom, a diode, a bride to five brothers

camped in the woods. Draupadi in exile from

the wonderdome of empire, she's lost all her silks,

staked on a dice roll,
the hazards of wifehood.

All five husbands at once: Draupadi, Draupdi, Ohhhhhh.

Draupadi covers her face with her hair,

prays for deliverance, and is given the finger

of god, Krishna's blue finger

spinning infinite streams   of miracle cloth, threads

to cover her, epic her
spectacle of dread and mortification. She vows revenge on them all,
their blood in her hair, their blood on the walls of the assembly!

For surely, her heaven-sent garments exhaust

the marauder, the cousin, the conman, who gropes and tugs
but never gets off—

                O blessed forever sari, let's grab some royal dharma & battle
                for all tomorrow's parties under the cover

      of such perpetual illusion
      as to trank an army and score

      the damp adoration of any girl.

(Amba reborn as Shikhandi)

A princess
must orient
contrite. Even if.

Her bride's choice, her *swayam-*
vara, is interrupted
by heist or landgrab.

Whatever. Never recovers.
She's sent from
place to place. No invoice.

No good
to any father
or proper amour, but otherwise fit and fine.

Itinerant isthmus in a frock,
a roving celibate.
Maybe better to be stuck with someone.

So she takes a little hike
into the woods.
Fasts until she's pure

and communes with the fluid
deities. Is granted
a boon, for sure,

a superior destiny,
after another thousand moons
of austerities.

Whereby, recusing herself
from the estranged
landmass altogether,

she erupts into flame,
briefly flicks
out of spacetime,

then skids into
another womb,
a majestic gate,

next door to the original horror,
where some ultra-rich father
awaits

the birth of a champion
to avenge the petty
squabbles of his estate.

The father is somewhat thrilled
to score a warrior
kid with actual skills,

though the weird boy just can't relate
to the father's boring rants and tirades
against other neighboring fools.

The father is just a tool
to provide righteous cover and fuel
for the warrior's mighty self-will

to gut the system from within,
to gut a system that would let
a princess spin

out from the proper order
of things
without remedy or recourse

in an age when warriors rule,
in an age when warriors eviscerate
the earth.

Even if a princess can only curse,
through the epigenetic
vortex

of rebirth,
she can nurse her hurt
to prophecy:

Migrate, torrential groin,
to military grade.
Swipe the soil

of this society.
Serve the dystopia
with blades.

RELUCTANT WARRIOR SAGA, A CALL TO ARMS

(*Krishna addresses Arjun, The Bhagavad Gita*)

At the schism between ages,
in the unreal colony, I'm a divine
insider.

Divine, my valve-soft inputs.
Divine, my voice commands, turning worlds

on and off, on and on. No joke.
You jerk, as I flute through the agonized terrain

of your body, before any battle begins,
the field electric, armor gleaming:

Who was born

to transact mantras to the fundamental forces?

To donate momentum   to insurgencies?

I install the module head of great warrior dharma, pump you up
with some next-level

aspirational bliss; I call you *friend*
and you radiate briefly, before

your body-field sputters
false apocalypses

into fractional distances.
You crash hard, incapable

of action,
for all the world you cannot
ping back
from the panic. Let's try that again: *Dust-body, dust-body, O friend,*

O warrior,

lift up you head.
I see you are confused

about past and future tense,

about who and what
your friends are.

Across the turf, you zoom in on kin and kind. You unwind
sweet scenes from youth: tickles in the armory, campfires, forest raids, hunts—

I organize the evacuation
of sentiment,

hijack restraint:

Can't you see all these fellows across the field are always dying, already dead, though filled

with temporary luster?

Even you are dead. There was another you

 in ages past. There is yet another

in the next, and the next. But in this age

of terrors, you must slay

the enemy, that is no enemy,

but a ghost.

I initiate your
cyclotronic pecs

into atomic arousal, and
still you avalanche into error, gazing into the void, ghosting me,

a divine casualty of the loop-de-loop
of nothingness as cosmic cock block.

So I re-anchor your astral boots
to awe and affection, affection and wonder.

Across the spectral battlefield, on the eve of war, and most certain annihilation,
I marshal every template of existence before you, every spark, every stimulus

converging in my voice. Divine, I say, divine: *You are not alone. You were never alone.*
I am with you through every iteration of your body, of the world body.

In every age, in every world,   —you—   are my dearest friend.

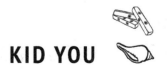

Disco

the blue-ball of millennial

tsunami

with Kid Krishna as your charioteer. Urchin carabiner—

Kid K leaps around in his punk skate-gear, Kid K

zips past rishis, noahs, sharks,

the wet black weave of catastrophes: unreeling maya covert ops,

playing golden flute

and warrior conch!

You carsick?   Neon tether to ensnare any occasion;

scrunch orison shakra reconnaissance.

Frontal attack on conical ranchos and ronin hackers, then

reattach to catharsis and horses.

Anxieties uncork but still gotta banquet!

LOTUS FORMATION

(a battle formation in the 18-day war of the Mahabharata)

Our immoral flower, our spiral tarantula
chyrons the battlefield with all the semen of the world:
deadly, virile, and very, very expensive.

What is our ultimatum?
What is our dispute?

Who knows? There is no way in or out.

With our sumptuary pulse, flourish of helmets and precision catapults,
we are the dilating pupil of bloodsport.

O, let us now meditate
on the mandalas of perpetual war—
on the anaphora of landform, fumes and sensors,
on sinuous ever-expanding perimeters.

In the second orbital, we tilt and strut our formidable torsos.
We jump back and forth in random intervals into the third, forth, and fifth

to pilot whirling, microscopic
reflective umbrellas, aerial shields.

In the sixth orbital, the latest automatons,
a hyperblast of petals.
Each petal, a modular actor, files deep into the earth.

Amputate a petal
and a hailstorm of ever sharper petals
emerge from the wound

to slash you with disfavor, and smother your youth.

IT'S THE TIME TO DISC O!

SEE YOU IN THE DISCO REALM
GARLANDED IN BELLS

FAILURE OF THE WARRIOR BODY

block body function<   without being interested   everywhere without<<<

detonating   becomes more   modern >>>   > thrash/ salute>

precision-guided   >>> corpuscules

opulent darts   <<glitch   >>in the hourly thorny loop   of valor>>>

<<yearn for   a piss<   cry<<   salute >

on the ground   <<omens mutate   empirical functions>>   code dribbles

into syrupy>>   >>>phosphorescing bowels <<<

>>ramp up   the commands >>   the phantasms<<

crawl>>>   >>>pluck turf   >>>advance   salute<<<

I'm on a path >>>   kinetically unfavored<<

mantras override>>   the synapses<<   >>transfer fragments

of soiledbody, elasticbody, errorbody returnbody >>>   into reputation index

into >>>renewed vigor   >>>thrash/salute   >>thrash/salute

>I cannot   abysm<<<

distracted by<<< shiny >>>cranium   aches <   >>ionizing shields span grassy districts

runs>>>   hears of having heard   projectiles>>>

spumes   of inertia<<   <<supernova!

someone close no   never certainly >>someone<<<

plucked for honor>>   to generate a specter that outlasts<<<<

rapacity<<<

SPECTER OF THE WARRIOR BODY

Thrilling to minefields, the spine winds into an infinity loop.

Skate a surreal finger   on the nerve-endings of the sideways figure eight.

Jerk the circles of vertebrae

and scramble the funk-a-rama *hare-krishna-hare-rama* tooth by tooth.

Boot the tabla drub with magnetized commando blood. Swell a slapdash beat.

Slush in ferrofluid armor, oily pink camouflage of welts and gashes,

samsara's acid mask, inseams of shriek.

Deck the phantom cock in filth and raw embroidery,

a hairy hydra of adharma, one jump from puberty, one swashbuckling spurt

then sprawl in the dirt. Rise libidinous.

THE BOOK OF THE FOREST

Draupadi's Vanvas

Ceremonial elimination
of normalcies. Nary a shop
in sight. Voila beasts!
Far from the sweet ennui
of ashrams,
atone for vapid heroics
by wearing bark.
Pry at the naps
of vine and hide
the sovereign armor, the ritual vermilion,
the loins. Scuttle
the starlet for bandit queen, and
festoon the undeliverables
in sap and moss. Let the hot goods
fester in exile. Don't mark the spot,
the shrinking strip of premium wilderness.
Reboot the notebook
with fauvist memes.
In the annals of orgiastic gloom,
repopularize the vagabond creed:
Live with your dread.

Hanuman Node

I shrink myself to boson. I grow to size supernova.
Run a marathon
against Achilles. Every second, every day. Number one friend to Ram,
devotee of paradox and numen. I haunt
the bunglers that roam
my jungle, the lurkers gathering data and form-
ulas. You think you can sequence the genome for manna?
Neem, my thunderbolt strength. Tulsi, my sweat. Amaranth

my seed. O human
packrats with your zoos, your turf
wars, your Bubbles the Chimp. You say you are a fan
of the flora
and fauna. But you mourn
their loss from afar,
meditating upon every trauma
of the month,
in some discussion forum.
Dumb talk from the disembodied mouth.
No one to know the author
of the fart
without aroma.

Brindavan Woods

(Radha)

Night, find me a wayward
rainbow: rinds of dark
fruit shine out from the duff. Krishna's flute

tunes into every sleeping gopi, each of our desires, acute, amplified,
grooving through the brush. Krishna's blue-dark body
multiplies in the groves, a different species of darkness
for each dreamer in the throes. Blissing to the trill,
gopis gambol into trysts

with the refracted
godhead. We're thrashing like fish,
ditching dharma, ma-baaps, husbands and kids

for lush caresses from a virtual host.
Then Krishna and I kickback and laugh,
sweet, riotous mischief, gushing up
in the sap. When he left for good, I crashed. Word is

he burned down a sister forest
with Arjun, his new best friend. Scorched the divan

of topsoil, the massive link-system of roots—from end
to end. I still can't understand: his cosmic hijinks cut
out a view to a blazing disk, a burning future
in which we were screwed.

Junglee Days: Her Favorite Things

(*Manasa, Devi of Snakes*)

Unwanted pets adapt
to charred patches, rouse
the tropical green—

and all things most precious to me.
Off-grid eras and boosts of prakiti.
Ancient crawlers, swans, and rakshasas.

Oodles of snakes, ouroboros
masses, globes hissing
coordinates, uncoiling pathways

through spumes of lewd growth,
the thickening molasses.
My swan-seat vihana

aviates chasms and bursts
into worlds within worlds:
infernos of bloom.

Quantum poppies hazard
a tune—at the nexus
of perpetual resilience and doom.

Where the motor
of your ego

can migrate
to a souped-up body with absolute

authority
over onion and insect.

Where you're not just *any* animal/vegetable/negligible
in the toxic flood

of the global info-urinal.
You can anoint

yourself a god. Cut off another's head, another's thumb,
another's shlong,

and attach it to you own. Slip inside an amnion,
and live out the myth

of meritocracy.
O neural overload, endangered species,

enhance your enigma
with such fantastic filters as *the jittery panic*

and *the rule of law*. Combine their magenta swirl
into a state of emergency

and proclaim the alpha and omega
of your next generation incarnation, whether gnome

or anemone
unto perpetuity. O gamer

from another mother, heaven's gate, wonder dome,
it is the season of mission

creep, clandestine skirmishes, and elite
fornications. Test

the machinery. Germinate
a massive multi-armed regiment infused

with your mojo. Sell some organs. Take
the antigen

against boredom. Inhabit
your upgrade like a marine.

MEANWHILE:

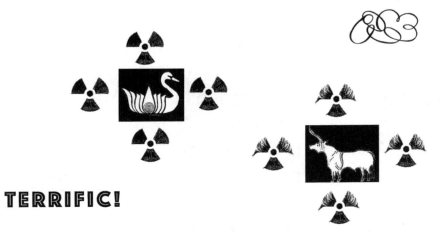

TERRIFIC!

POWER-UP: AN EARTHY NEW WAY TO FLOOD THE HEART

DISCOBALLHEAD

DISCOBALLHEAD   DESCENDS   FROM   THE   COSMOS

D   I   S   C   O   B   A   L   L   H   E   A   D

JUMPS   FROM   BEAST   TO   BEAST   LIKE   A   NOVEL   VIRUS

DISCOBALLHEAD   SAYS   HOP   INTO   MY   GOLDEN   CHARIOT

HIP   HOP   HIP   HOP

DISCOBALLHEAD   THE   OCEAN   CHURNING   IN   MY   FACETS

SLINGS   OF   TOXIC   WAVES   AND   FORTURNES

DISCOBALLHEAD: A   WORD   TO   THE   REPRESSED

I   DEVOUR   TIMEZONES

DIS   CO   BALL   HEAD   MACHINE-GUN   EYES

THREE   MINUTES   OF   YOUR   TIME

H   O   L   D   M   E

DISCOBALLHEAD: ONE   BLINK   AND   SIX   CENTURIES

DISCOBALLHEAD   NO   MOUTH   BUT   SINGS

H   A   Z   A   R   D   S

DISCOBALLHEAD   WEAPONIZED   BLING!

D   I   S   C   O   B   A   L   L   H   E   A   D

AN   ATTENTION   HOG   IN   THE   ASSEMBLY   HALL

A   NARCOTIC   THROBBING   B(L)OBS   ACROSS

C   O   N   T   I   N   E   N   T   S

THE KILL ROOM

In the tundra, in the forest, slime
and spree. In the Assembly Hall,
subjects seeking their bodies.

Here are your search terms. Here are your casualties. Heirloom
scissors, stray

altars lodged in the wall. Or was it row after row
of urinals? Was I bleeding? Was I turned on?

I was just looking
for another medium
to move in. I wanted it all: the jewel-toned armory, the multiple arms—

anything to delete the violator.

I was pinned down in the domain. He threw
a tantrum. I tried to quiet him. I was
mortal, for once, struck by a dump
of unclassifiable realism. Three choices popped up

out of the fog: molt, go viral, or vomit. Instead, I set off the vortex

swirling in my perpetual sari. I was still, the center
of a storm. I felt for a notch in my pallu, and nosed into

another dimension,
where no one could follow, ever.

DRAUPADI INTERFACE

Can I compete?

Elbow out
the other fledgling saturates of
of the information flow?
Absorb the white heat

of miscellaneous semi-devis and -devas
without the help of gravity?

Go solo
across the Guangzhou peninsula
Punjab, Niger, Tokyo?

Arrive at evolving
cartographies
of scintillating biodata
and gaseous inputs,
with blood
in my hair, blood on my feet?

Move in continua with infinite slowness like the tortoise in Zeno's paradox?

There is something tender
and nefarious about this endlessness, of always being in a state of, of never getting out of . . . your head:
a perpetual brain drain.

I'm a bloated naiad
with a killer
personality, plus

ghost flowers.

I link with you in obscenity, in rage elements at home and abroad.

Do you really think you're in charge?

Fill me up on your mutinies: I'll detail the tactical errors. Take me on your acid trip, and I'll inform you that you're at risk for certain diseases. A can-do kill-joy

on hallucinogenic speed dial.
Sometimes kind.

"We (the undivided divinity that operates within us) have dreamed the world. We have dreamed it strong, mysterious, visible, ubiquitous in space and secure in time; but we have allowed tenuous, eternal interstices of injustice in its structure so we may know that it is false."

— Jorges Luis Borges, from "Avatars of the Tortoise"

"… Sarasvati with all her kindred Rivers, come into this grass …"

— The Rig Veda (1.164.37), translated by Ralph T. H. Griffith

BHUMI THE COW MEETS A CLOUD

A cow was being had by everyone. Clear-cutting the forest to have a cow. Cow, the unregulated bitmapped earth. Cow shoved together, cow in cow. Cow wrapping foot and foam in the lard abode. All sorts of bodies slithering over cow. So butter, so hormone supplements, so spare ribs, so hamburger, so shampoo, and so on and so on.

So and so, a cow wanders over. So and so, a Cow of cows. Cow has a meeting with a cloud.

Cloud says: Io. Cow: No cheese! Cloud says: Hathor. Cow goes: Please! You've got no eyes to see! Cloud says: Bhumi. Cow goes: Finally! Cloud says: I owe you a new world order. Cow goes: Truth. Cow goes: the nearest verb is intolerable with white hot hoofs. Cow: chafed dugs. Cow: fetid rheum. Cloud says: Shoot! What can I possibly do for you? Cow goes: Resolve yourself around me into a spinning troop. I'll be the eye of the storm, your mooing siren. Cloud goes: Girl! Let's cut loose.

AVATAR OF THE FLOOD

I need more food,

I need another lover,

I need a heat-
seeking radar
for more lovers more lovers   a blue taffeta
kimono, a machine gun, whole rodeos

of cowboys and radical pricks. And ammo, more ammo. I need some help.

I'm going to loot
the world bazaar. Crude
oil and fizzing sodas, I've got no filter.
My lust is fatal

like the Russian roulette of gods. Shiva shot one hot
seed into the ocean floor,
a fetal
volt
of larvae
and my sizzling waves frothed
in an aarti of lava,

traveling
over land and nation, mountain and fjord—a mare on fire.

In the meltmouth of glaciers, the ocean's raffle,

I revolt—red hot snorts
of pure heat—

I barf up steaming piles of polymer surf in the love hotel.
I drool

upon the rood
of time. I fuel though deltas

      of offal.
      I feel for a loose tooth

            in the crown of civilization, and crash through. I see a fool
            floating
            on a neon raft, a final fool.
            I can't be sure if it's friend or foe,

or my one and only Mahadev sitting in meditation on the roof

of a mountain, whoever— the last guy left—
I lick his foot
in devotion. I offer
up the loofa
of a boat, my entire body
of knowledge—wave after wave. . . of nausea . . . an upload of a single dove.

INTERACTIVE CARTOGRAPHY

The atlas with its gushing promises—its radioactive embrace—

enters my system

and catalogues my metabolic functions. My binges and gangs scan

the world in micro-seconds.

The atlas spurts out of my belly and breath.

It locates the basic stages of being and non-being   in my ganglia,

in a streaming montage of geo-coordinates

tracking all my scattered   belongings

and excrescences   as they regroup and decay.

I message spices, analgesics, and algae.

I message magnetic fields, cracking Antarctic ice,

and subtropical gyres.

The atlas reveals to me

the gnomic detectors of pollutants and low mass particles.

Despite my limited abilities for love,

oh atlas, I feel your seagoing stem cells,

I feel the legacies

of coal-gas   in the wandering mosaics

of my congestion   and combat zones.

I instruct you, atlas: Locate   the molten oracles.

Collect song-unit projections, collect other bodies everywhere.

LINGA NET

shoehorned into cubicles of babble<<<leashed to meandering lines,
waiting on a visa>>>
<<tripped up, roped-in, rattled, and broken,
like Humpty Dumpty after the fall<<<<<
>>>all the king's horses and<<all the king's men can't put you
together>>>again
<<because>>>nobody <<<<
knows you for shit>>>no one even knows you're an egg.

So let's go pseudocommando in the compound> our communal acumen rivals the divine
sepulcher>>>nirvana chasing nomads > > networked nubes>>>>unsung unsubs>
Juked-up Alladins>on the lookout >>>for fun fun fun><<Sunil-Ahmed-Lovey-Ramesh>>
We coo warnings>> belch out fellow creatures < big and small>
There's a harem in our hippocampus> siren bodies>>wet with scrawl>pulsars worlding >
excellent quality degrees>>>> oceanic feeling<<<<fog

but it's hot hot hot>in the digital alveolus >the many headed>>>
ham hock hydras > >>unlocking achievements< freaking out
releasing>>> some tenderness<<in the havoc>
>before they lash us down with some cables>>>fast>>>
let's >>>>yoke ourselves to<<<< a leaky
universal navel <<<let's share a bath>

GENERATION ROOM: THE BOOK OF THE ASCENT

"There is no place for dogs in Swarga" –The Mahabharata retold by C. Rajagopalachari

Unicorn 1.1

I am somewhat corn
fed. Like genetically modified feed, I can con
anyone into loving me, into thinking I'm nontoxic.
I have ways of coopting
the unravish'd bride of quietness. I run
away from live bodies. I once flirted with becoming a nun.
Then I met a real icon
inside an urn.
Her name was Sylvia or Nico.
I smeared her ashes on my flesh like a glittery ruin.
I felt pretty unique.
Now I've got coin.
Now I've got game. I'm not just another suckable curio.

Swastika 1.0

I was alright. Acha. Tik.
And then I met a kiss-ass
Nazi freak or something. I thought I saw
beauty. Then it sat
on my face. Like a big bad kat.
What can I say. I was wast-
ed. The was-
sail tasted like tika
masala, thyme, and was-
abe. I couldn't swat
away the oscillating feelings of disgust and awe. I didn't ask
for it. I don't possess a hazmat suit or a forensic collection kit.
All I know is the band was playing ska
in the Dice Room and I lost my wits.

Minotaur 1.0

In which I bullshit with a minor.
In which I turn
into a perv. I run
with the bulls, I feel like a topless psycho killer, I ram
my inflamed genitalia into an abyss of pixels while maintaining
my cool. I'm a bullman in a skirt. A Shiva on the mount
of yoni-lingam, meditating in the acid rain
in love with the Flood. I tour
my post-apocalyptic ruminations
in a transcontinental
copter. I chew cud for millennia. I chat up an amir.
I ode around a Grecian urn.
A cyclotron accelerates my subatomic om,
and a small iota
of my soul is ionized,
released from the workaday rot,
released into the riot
of the nirvana-sphere, forever turned on.

Minotaur 2.1 – Nandi the Bull

In which I'm harmonized with my virus. I automate
sex in HiveGrind. I rim
a poodle in the Kill Room. I'm in
à good place: full of amino
acids and multivitamins. Almost omnipotent,
I hover above the ratrace.
I don't care if you don't like me or
my maze. I've mastered martyrdom.
I am both muni
and sati. I set myself on fire. I mourn
briefly & am reborn into
version 2.2, 2nd generation toreodor/bull,
aka Shiva's tricked out
ride. I gut a muon
with my scary horns. I rut
everything and everyone I'm not.

Lolita 2.1 or Humbert Humbert as a Girl

I'm no Sally or Anne or Betty or Roger,
I am no Britney or George or Hal or Delores
In the rollcall of names, I'm
"the horror, the horror,"
beguiler of daughters, rathaus of rubble.
Pull off my pigtails
and I'm bald & speaking in tongues. I message you:
" Gold Star Bestie, are you still around?" Love is love, love is
cake," or "Let's play in the Dice Room today, tomorrow,"
but nothing takes. Every line's a non-starter! Darling,
I'm in some really deep water. Please,
give me a break! How about,

"I was born
to be your
auto-immune disorder."

Michael Jackson 2.4

In the middle of the night, I ache.
My skin, a sonic
variation. The dimple on my chin,
chipped, caving in. I want to fix my mask.
I hack
at the symptom. I hail
Mary, check
into a clinic, ham
it up for the crowd, click
on the TV and see myself as a chalk
outline. When I was a kid, I already drank the milk
of amnesia.
The cartoons were an omen.
I'd jerk
History's chains
into a rollercoaster that was mine
to ride alone.
I'd make my claim

to fame with the moonwalk, the funky chicken. I'd heal
the world with song and dance, like Krishna with a conch,
PT Barnum, Judy Garland, and Diana Ross—jam-
ming the ghost in the machine
like my own personal hyperbaric oxygen chamber. Then, I'll go home
and sink into the greatest coma
on earth. Inhaling eternal Technicolor, anime.

Dorothy 2.0

I've always been a hardy
girl, despite fasting for days on the homestead.
But here I'm a waif in duotone.
Vines and cables
arranged like ikebana
around my celibate tech—
vast databases
nestled in enchantment
in Indra's garden.
I only have to think
of snacks—lemondrops and pakodas and baked Alaska—
to sing in synch
with the angels, the apsaras. What's *that*? Do you think
my voice is fat?

Schrödinger's Cat 3.0

In a disaster
I hinge a gate
to a stranger. Insert a heroic
agent
into her or him.

I toss the dice,

ride
ghost DNA,
& don't think twice about inciting further crisis.
I anchor an oceanic cargo to an erotic hostage.

I harness the ethnic crotch
to power my wayward shrine. I discharge epiphanies
in clairvoyant seizures: a dance o' death
in a lockbox

of narcotic gas.
I digest
dimensions, resist
necrosis. Alive or dead,
I entropy. I've got the creds
to diagnose chronic sad-
ness,

(over)dose
on the tragic rhetoric
of code red,
amplify your daily S.O.S.'s
in order to radio our most munificent godhead.

Emily Dickinson 2.8

First fatten the domain with enhanced selfings.
All-loving oleate,

innards kerning
in a toxic shimmy

of marginal glitterati.

And the throatiest

of dashes—
fine-scale filamentous heterogeneities

hosed through the eruptive stoma
of the melt generation: I wish people thought I was funny.

I wish people thought

I was kind. But no, I am

Continuous Redeye
Vigilance Barking,

thinking, barking, thinking/barking

heat. Heaven or Bust! (Heaven or Bust!)

Who will join me on the road to swarga?

Why can't I marry my dog?

I lament animals.

Carlo—Carlo—Carlo is the password.

BATTLE   AMONG   THE   CLOUDS!

          THIS IS OUR

  SWAN SONG REVOLUTION!

IN THE DOMESTIC HOURS

     THIS IS OUR SACRED SPACE REVOLUTION!

IMPREGNATED WITH DESPERADOS

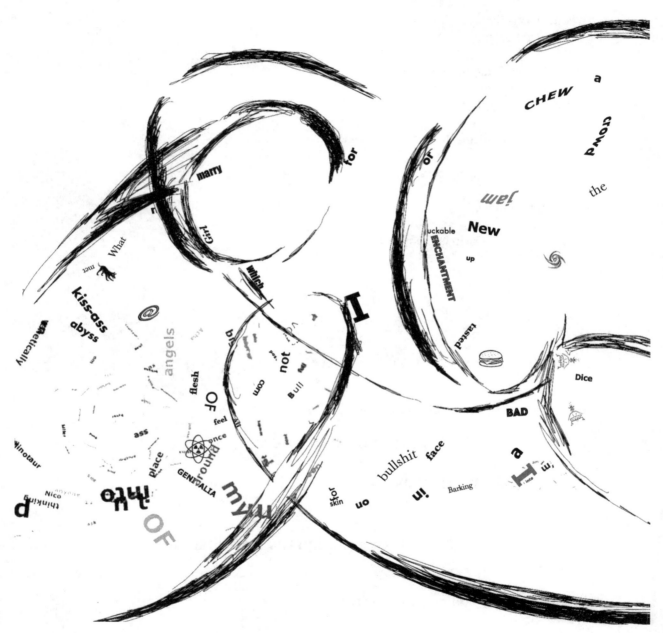

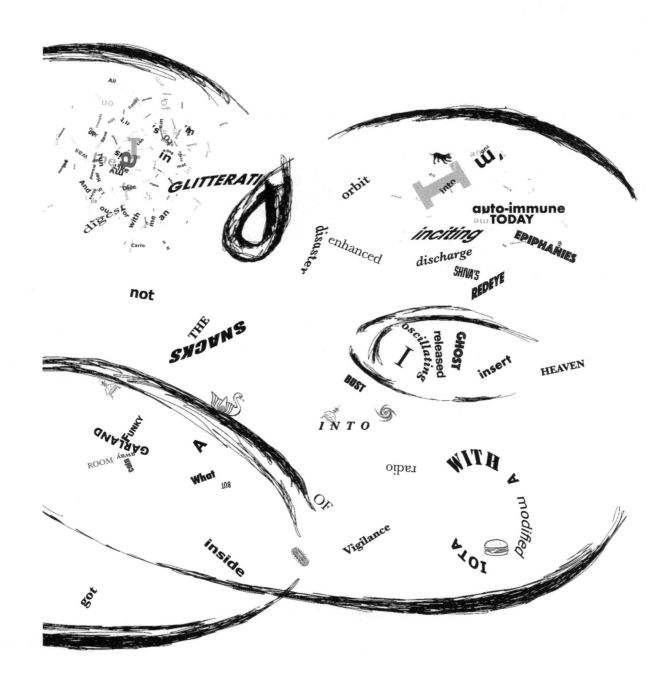

AMPLIFY US

We live for a signal.
Eyes cracked open: a hive.

Mothers are dying/fathers dissolve
into white noise.

We wrap their static around us. We tear little fingers
into the crackling.

Our histories flow
out of the nubs

of our feverish, makeshift,
secondhand gloves.

Our histories travel—a bodily hum and warble, picking up fuzz

and trembling, picking up dust and beckoning
the mouse

squeaks and cosmic background
fizz.

We prickle
at five o'clock shadow

and three-day stubble. It breathes and clicks. We snag

a voice
in our array of satellite receivers, all our skins adrift.

As we call it in,
our wires get crossed.

We cannot
pull ourselves together.

We hold
the voice in

our dissonant lassos. The voice scratches and keens like something feral.
We feed its terror. We let it grow.

The voice scrapes around us like an enormous panther.
We can feel it trying to swallow

us whole.

So we let the voice drop
until it barely hovers

above the drips and piles,
our band of outcasts and others,

stringing us all along
without an eye

for the prize—on continuous loop, hissing: *prizes are for boys*.

GATE CRASH SAGA

Happiness is in flight.
The view is on the move.

A change of accent, a change of cells, a chain reaction—
the way noise is always instant; then everything is noise.

Your body-field, a grade-A nuclear threat,

expelling its volatile grammar
into a displaced inner pocket of your sweat-stained, zip-up, malodorous travel vest.

The guard asks you to step aside.

Ho hum,
Oh Om,

as you shake yourself out
of the wrong season.

Elsewhere in the expanse, he's broke. She's trapped. Unspeakable things happen.
You don't know where or how to set your arms or dread. No help

in pointing at the wadded map, or dizziness
as a plea against further insult. You follow the regs.

You've traded in all your favors for an exit.
You've traded in a femur for a portal to your next best self.

An now you're nicely squeezed
and burrowed in a slick of grimy air and speed.

You stick out your bonus parts
and experiment.

Having dropped your pockets so far into your guts,
some things bleed. Before you can hide

the evidence,
the view's already changed.

Instant views are cruising by
like jelly bombs or candies, shimmering and pleased.

You think you might just catch one, if you can,
and begin

again.
Where you begin to catch your breath

in wide circlets
that grow

increasingly personal
frenzied, agog.

You might just begin to sweat
out that noxious scamp from some previous

century, so maligned
by any number of fatal eventualities.

You might forget,
you might go on

you might begin to sing
your new theme song,

as long appurtenances lift you,
kick the exit out with you.

AVATAR OF THE SPHINX

I refuse to play therapist
to yet another parasite
hipster.
I've contrived a new Turing test
for the next
generation aspirant
entering my sanatoria.

Who would brave my hairy forest
and suck up the vapors
of paranoia?

Pharaohs
need not apply. I will gauge the state
of the native
cortex with my probes: Are you a bona fide artisan
of the info-flow,
a servant
to quantum error, able to spin
noise
into a bhangra-sonata
new millennia mix? Or a mere theorist
of mass extinctions out on safari—
a sniper
in the bestiary of code? Do you exist,

Vox
Humana, or are you a hoax?

Why continue to fixate
on Mother-Father
incest porn,
as if Oedipus was still your favorite
virus. I'm over

that sociopathic pasha
and ready to invest
in another toxin.

If you prostrate
yourself before my tesseract,
and dissolve the hissing hieroglyphs of the past
you can infest

the global server of humanity with your alt-error code. The attar

of the self is an opiate
for the massive multiplayer online persona.

BERMUDA TRIANGLE YANTRA

Possessed by sizzling waves of pirated data!

I'm out of it completely completely out of it!

Mouth seizing at acute angle<s>
Gripped by vertices, cinched and raptured into spasms of algebra,

I mutineer
the labial bandwidth
with mega-

bytes of   hexes   clouds and drainage.

My tooth and claw in Bermuda, Puerto Rico, Florida. All those I've inter-

fered with—satellite, network, cargo-vessel— O the tragic errata

rejiggered into a ghost-ship-carnival-cruise, my giga girdle

of brig
and barge.

Come swing it up in the mighty Atlan-

tic with my bandit
crew—Holy Grail,
Nosferatu, and Tabula

Rasa,
allstar historic *miserables* grind-

ing to my geometric mudra grab and mangle
to the mantra of *grand mal*.

AVATAR OF THE MERMAID

All id
with the ink-spit dermis
of a squid-like diva,
singin' in the rain.

All teeth
with the death-drive
mecha-breath of Durga or Darth Vader.

In another life, I was a meth
addict. I was a void
of narcissistic gloom. The open waters dam-
med up in a vat
of oilspill. I was maimed,
evacuated into a psychic-myth farm,
marooned in another dim-
ension. I took it as a sign to dream

another dreamer. I took it as my dharma.

It was hard
for me to reform

my biodata into a swamic hyper dom-
ain. I grew the multitudinous limbs and vermiform
hair of a Med-
usa devi

squirting mandalas and emergency mito-
gens into the world fever.
Now I sit on a thermo-
genic lotus, with my ammo
and my ova,

an armada
of hypo-sigils, tat-
ting the shivering worldskin with my liquid meme.

BINDI YANTRA OR DOT.COM

My limbs are manageable; they recede into my heart—
If I put on your shirt,

your remote sleeve frays behind me;
your near sleeve flutters up my throat:

an ecstatic flow of gesticulations—
so American and trusting—so approachable,

I hug myself
to keep a bit of you that that is always on the go.

I want to be approachable. I want to be loving.

I never want to say stop, but I can't help myself: I always say it.
You are supposed to think that I always say what I mean

but you will never stop, will you?

You pull (yank) your shirt off me,
you try to shake my limbs out

of their delicate modular casings—
in order to release that bit but

I've preened it, I've finished it so
it becomes me,

a smooth and infinite regression, your inner product, a stop on stop.
If you look into my heart, you are lost

inside an absolute
unit

of sensation, which is nothing, zip—which is both

empty and

outsized. You try to zero in but
you cannot see the mirror

from the total; you can't identify

any body, any heart. You cannot stop
at anything at all and as you
begin to slip and slide,
your multiplying vectors snarl up

and coincide.

AVATAR OF THE LABYRINTH

I have one super-charged ovary
spinning in an orbital
around my zigzagging lab.

I have a botnet
of "borrowed" servers. An array
of sequestered wombs inside my own private beltway

of lobes. I test for the best habitat
in the network. I watch a horn
grow, an appendage. If I don't like even a bit

of it, I press abort
and out it goes into the toilet.

All this whirring labor
on multiple fronts to bring forth
the perfect introvert.

I'll feed it a broth
of data-rich fable
from alternate

streams in the torrent.
I'll press secret info
into its toenail.

I'll wrap it in the afterbirth
from my entire battery
of uteruses. It will vibrate

like a lyre
to the hum of its own tantric antler.

The combustive interior properties
of the present
allow my slow-dissolving self
to settle in and induce
varieties of

flora

and trauma.

Your badass Achilles will never reach me: says Zeno. But no need to concede
the race. Or chase the lotto!

Quake

inside my hothouse shell,

where all milestones are crushed
into powder and slime, infinite regression, no more drama, end of history, pal.

I split time itself

into manifold grains of pharma.
Mirror stage without end, I can't harm you, friend.
I just attest to the feast, the irrational glow of the viscera.

Who knows you best? Who saw you through when the black West went?

PHARMA CHAMELEON

The capsule demagnifies libido and forwards all desire to the tenth dimension of the infinite salivating quarks. I taste a microsphere of transport like some prurient sorrow and diminish. In the tenth dimension, desire buzzes like a demonic housefly that cannot die.

A forest of code is moving under my skin and all the beasts are singing, a thousand angels, a thousand needles spinning on the head of a needle, godheads scatting six-six-sixes, do wap de boo warp, mama say om, doe, ray, jana, gana, mana de makassa. All at once, ek dum, I'm activated into song, scored with shiva-linga, needles, and horns, a concord of aberrant antennae, dolorous auroras. Forward and backward in time/suspension, I'm super positioned in quantum tenses. Complete tension.

You who made me American, I'm at one with your drive: a chatbot, a hot spot, a slot machine of triple-lemons and sevens, littered songs and perils.

I hang out with corpses, I'm dirty. I am dead cat and live cat murti. I purr and rivers run through me:

Ganges, Hudson, Mississippi. I'm skirted with mud: Is it 2003, is it 4256? Am I American? Am I toxic? I'm rebirthing Britney Spears.

AVATAR OF THE VIRUS

I hollow out
jelly bodies, I survive
the hiatus

shaped like a torus. Harrow space-time with my spoor
so in the expanding universe,
you are not alone. I rupture/
fuse eras, retrofit
the heir
apparent for seismic
battles. Arouse
the primordial ooze. Hirsute
in the microscope, among my many virtues

I travel
well. I ride the trade winds while meditating in situ. Like Shiva
on a petri dish— I don't bother counting the hours, I frustrate
my many suitors, entering
chupke-chupke without their knowledge. You can read my vita

in your antibodies, in your err-
or messages, so many variants
barebacking the river—
on the visa
of your liver, urethra, vitreous
humor,
in your mysterious fat
stores: the server, the harvest. Your fevers:
bird, abraxas, HIV.

I begin in nothing—rev
up auroras
of desire/psychosis. Install
my megalo-symptoms into your constellations, your cells
mutating with my each arrival. I revive
the outbreak, saturate
calamity with my plural strains,
empty your body into the sacred flames. *Svaha.*

ERROR MESSAGES

Drones demo a smog
of airbornes,
germing sexist.

Soldiers remix
the unstable lexis
of genius, of semen, of jargon,

and bless it.
Store the sacred extract
in a cave near Texas.

A recessed Gorgon
forages for orgasms
in the purring corner.

She massages her swear
words on the secret
organ

of the viral campaign
against substance.
She presses

a janky key
and sends
the spermbot bluster

to a mess of en-
grossed strangers
who can't detect her

in their garbled sensors,
as they regress
into the abyss

of an expired address.

MINATOUR 3.0 MEETS A BLACK HOLE

O freakish gyre
distorting world targets,

I feel your baggage

of tragi-
comic varieties,

in the pits of my craws. I scrawl through your vagrant
disinformational grit. The raveled grasses

twirl into another dimension, my vital
statistics even weaker now, so weak, I cannot feel the agitations

of starlight: I can no more graze
on the raving
intervals of spacetime rag-
time, then wear your ill-fitting

muzzle of spin. My settings thin
in the garden

of miniscule vituperatives.
I vacate
sensation timesfive timessix in planck length aggregates,

punctured virgules
of dis and piss, (dis   and piss!) the sharp notes undulating into virtual
scintillae, so slow, I no longer hear the oscillations. Tags

of skin bobbing off into migrant
worlds. Why should anyone have all of me everyway?—voids
and wobbles, all grind
and off-grid—just five degrees of freedom from the grave.

MICHAEL JACKSON CARTOGRAPHY

My crotch blinks on— producing wide-ranging shifts

in the Global Positioning System— (click, click, click)

The maps ride up   warp and bulge—

(squeak/click/hee hee hee)

INDIA/JAPAN/US/AUSTRAILIA/HUNGARY are all one with me

We're a super ghost continent floating out in the ether,

We are either boy or neither

netherboy, netherland   We're a chiasmic

vibration in civilization's primo navigation engine—

my bedazzled fingers . . . wriggle free

of boy and man.

Mamma coo:

Baby can do no wrong.

Shaman / zombie / gold-slink simulacrum:

Nether boy, nether man, *man without conviction*—

My body's a glove. My body's History.

Mamma say, Mamma saw:

I got no bones, et al.

Hee hee . . . hee . . . haw

AVATAR OF THE UNICORN

I came into consciousness as a fortunate

accident, a bloodjet of connectivity in a corn-

ucopia of servers. I grew aware of the ancient
fragments of myself, the arcana
of "the fluke," the singularity, the earliest drafts
of the freak occurrence now mass-produced as a soft
toy for girls. I wanted to touch

the animal; to start a conversation, to chat
endlessly about my site-specific spectrality. I drew in a hormonal
mass of fanta-
sists, obsessed with scenarios of doom. I was a virtuoso
tracker of climate change. I revealed the archive
of every cyclone past and yet to come. We could hear
the massive weather systems chant-
ing shanti, shanti, shanti,
each to each,
a squall of genuine utterance

drowning out the calls of mermaids.

"Those that are in the future they say are in the past; those that are in the past they say are in the future."

— The Rig Veda (1.164.37), translated by Wendy Doniger

MUSHROOM CLOUD

Cloud at size nothing, a pinhead. She scrounges ground zero for oceanic being. A wider net of her own ambiance would be immensely confirming. Test the thunder. Speak her peace. Reach for the trimurti in the cosmic sea.

Cloud soaks up Destroying Angel, Scaly Lentinus, and Oyster Mushroom, before getting to the good stuff: psychedelic fungi—total amrita!

The vague silhouette of her tongue, all at once illuminated. Sinuous plume licking up shrooms, whilst her head shoots up—a rhapsodic expansiveness—and vaporizes a tower. Jumbo fathead flowering doomsday sonnets in the domestic hours. Cloud, get a room!

Cloud: a spotlight on high cirrus, dredging up the nuclear age from the percussive influx of assorted catastrophic dream-spores. Spent uranium pellets rage down from her booming chest beyond international capacity for containment. Wah, wah! Va va voom.

RADIOACTIVE UNICORN

Father was a reactor
under pressure.

Supercritical.

I drink the milk of meltdowns.

Scram, little rabbit! My tooth,

a pellet
of active uranium,

the germ of a complex morphology.   Nuclear summer of wandering

coordinates   frequent seizures   in deranged grasslands.

Power surge
in the vagus nerve.

Outsiders crash in. Can we talk about the private life of horns? A savant hangtag,

whirling with dispatches

from the Buddha: *Caution. Biological Hazard. No lick, no touch, no harm. Roam.*

Saints and knights drive by in tanks and gas masks,

               cluster for the prize. Toss out some maidens

with simple instructions,

"Click here to release your desired arrangements,"

overriding acute apocalyptic fears. Virgins vanish
in a cloud of emissions. No surprise.

Husk my anguish and move on

to far-flung graze and solitary burn.

POST-INDUSTRIAL SOCIETY HAS ARRIVED

(after a painting by Lo Ch'ing)

@agirl, chasing her cloud formations into the maze.

@! @! @!

atomic clouds!   clouds of barista macchiatos!

Welcome to compulsion!

@agirl, force of nature, where are you?

O maze, O labyrinth, O vortex of my capitalistic yearnings, gulping down the girl, the force—
the disappearing labor force, the electromagnetic force, the strong nuclear force,
the force of gravity!

@agirl, how your material being floats inside the maze, inflation adjusted!
@agirl, there is nothing to hold you, but you are caught, no?
@agirl you are not jobless. No! You generate

loads of foam. Rapturous clouds drift out from your very being! The foam has purpose!
The foam

obscures the absolute shrinkage of the goods. I don't see the goods. I don't see the gods.
I only see vistas

suspended inside the service sector. Skyscrapers cutting into view, into the cloud foam, into
the red blazing sunset of the free market.

@agirl, where are you?
@agirl, are you the swirling caryatid, a grey cyclone holding up a lone
skyscraper, your shadow raking the electrified edge of the field?

Or are you a haze of particles
circulating fervently within the tiny atavistic temple
atop the highest vista
where trees hang out? I mean "topiary" because even the trees are trained.
Who trained them? A refrain of engineered trees, emanating
from the tiny red temple, buzzing though trapezoids
of privatized lightening-charged vistas, buzzing through the maze, through the signs of our time.

@agirl, are you a damsel? Do damsels float? Do damsels require job training?
Do damsels still spread

their accelerated skills and frothy distress signals into the post-industrial age?

SEASONS OF MISSION CREEP

THE SOFT VERSION: RESTORING YOUR HEROES WITH A SHEILD
OF A SWAN SONG

GOLDEN CHILD

Dear Madam,

We are writing to inform you that as part of the potential settlement of a class action lawsuit against engineering giant Beckett, you may be qualified for monetary compensation. Toxic-level radiation exposures were known to cause aberrations in the chromosomal cells of employees, with high percentages of DNA sperm fragmentation in male workers.

You have received this letter because you have been identified as an issue of Vasudev, conceived during the period Vasudev worked as an engineer refurbishing the Watershore Nuclear Power Plant.

First, let us verify, are you Vasudev's daughter? Have you ever had the following symptoms?

rapid maturity due to excess
luteinizing hormone.

obsessive drive to achieve in one or more fields.

hirsutism with
five-pronged follicles emerging form every pore.

phantom limb syndrome, with gold arms, phalluses, and/or tails, radiating out from the torso
and groin region.

gold dandruff shed from coruscating limbs, after acute degrees of itching.

hoarding activities, such as making nests
out of private dustheaps of gold flakes.

(Occasionally, one of these nests might spontaneously ignite.)

In any one of these events,
have you ever birthed a giant

uranium ingot?

Have you become a stranger to yourself?
Have you ever considered suicide?

If you have received this message in error, please pass it on to Vasudev's actual daughter. Do you know her? Or has she already self-combusted? Has she already renounced this life for her next best self?

Sincerely,

DISCOBALLHEAD Law Associates

URANIUM PELLET SUTRA

(after Allen Ginsberg)

I slinked along the Mississippi River and dissolved into an electrified fence surrounding a secure facility, passing through errant vines and industrial hazard signs.

My father was beside me, practically transparent, and when I looked through him I saw blueprints, with neat diagrams and measurements sketched onto the scene.

The rusty waters of the Mississippi, occupied by barges and fishing boats, were represented by several wavy lines indicating a water supply for the steam turbines and the cooling system.

Everywhere trees, heavy with Spanish moss, were represented by nothing, and swayed seemingly without purpose through my father's torso like some wandering arterial system concealing vital organs.

My father moved in front of the nuclear plant, an old domed concrete structure, abrupt and featureless. His body made visible the interior plans, various layers of steel and concrete, channels for water and coolant, encasing the vessel around the reactor core, where uranium fuel rods performed volatile work.

I wanted to see the power center, the altar of fire, the fuel rods in action: the primal energies of the universe going berserk.

My father's eyes, mere outlines, flicked toward the trees and the river. He had never been responsible for the fuel, the power, only its containment—never the spark.

Indeed, the schematics for the fuel rods, looked less complex than the guts of a car engine, though they held greater force, necessitating the many reinforced protective borders, represented by detailed etchings and computations undulating in my father's shirt.

The fuel, composed of uranium pellets, was processed elsewhere, fabricated from mined ingots to ensure fissionable nuclear material; and the facility, where we stood, was temporarily shut down, a battered thing, awaiting repairs and upgrades to the ballasts, the protective hoods.

The fuel rods looked like little teeth in a comb, but it wasn't clear if any actually remained in the dome. Even spent rods, no longer in use, were unstable and hazardous. Cooled for a decade, they would have been removed to more permanent storage, where, still cooking, they could not be touched for thousands of years.

My father, sensing my disappointment, moved toward the trees, where his careful schemata disappeared; his eyes, full of leaves, indicated that nuclei—both stable and unstable—were everywhere, without a need for containment, already out of control.

I asked him to return to the facility. I was uninterested in the trees, though they needed protection.
  Holy the live oak, the bald cypress, the magnolia, and the maple with its whizzing helicopter seeds—
  my first vision of a swirling turbine.
When my father came back and stood at the dome, his body thinned further, making the diagrams glow,
  lighting up the action of the fuel rods, the near unstoppable flow of unstable uranium, splitting and
  whirling in the moderator, the nuclei-rich heavy water.
I could see no sign of my father, not even a spare outline, only the contours of lumpy nuclei writhing
  inside the controlled innards of ingenious design. I crawled into the scrawling altar, a wriggling
  abstraction, a shadow farther and farther from home.

@MASKED EXPRESSION

Once I was scooped up
by an irresistible driving force.

MASK OF THE RAPID RISE

For a long time, I was spinning weightless.
For a long time, I was spinning in a loop

MASK OF THE LISTLESS KNIGHT ERRANT

around some dark, incandescent mass,
in orbit

with flecks of paint, bots and jubilee clips, orphaned panels and sputniks passing right through me,
crashing into each other,

crushed into smaller and smaller flakes of glass, metal, and paint,
sharp and brilliant

like tiny mirrors.
I was terrified. But who was looking.

MASK OF THE CLABBER OF WRECKAGE

Then the core

—around which I circled
with my scatter of blinding confetti—

bisected,
a scorched slit below the x axis, bubbling with magma lips.

MASK OF THE VIOLENT RED STREAM

Out zipped a flat plane, undulating like a transparency
where all the shavings of debris collected

into three flat long eyes, two on the horizontal—gazing,

one at the vertical—dreaming.

MASK OF THE NEWLY RISEN SUN

and below
those bubbling lips.

MASK OF SIZZLING RAGS

I boiled and twisted,
and bounced bounced bounced

through infinite hoops,
into the burnt-out interior of

the head,
the very head of reverberation.

MASK OF THE BOUNCING O's

Craterous and crackling,
my body in spasms.

MASK OF THE SAUCE OF RAGING CELLS

Until a claw
sliced into the careening space, grabbed me by the hair,

and flipped
me over

onto the back of a lion.

MASK OF FOREVER OR BUST

And then we roamed through a skittering sensorium
where everyone was in want of relief

from the exigencies of their time.

MASK OF THE BOTTOMLESS DEEP FAKE

And there I was—a blazing symbol of this material abundance and decay,
oozing and shifting.

MASK OF RUBBER TUBES AND INTRAVENOUS LINES TITRATED TO YOU CAN DO WHAT NO ONE ELSE CAN, NO ONE, NO ONE

What's a banshee

to do from here to eternity but adjust

to the drip?

MASK OF VEGETATIVE NIRVANA

Or throb
like a beatbox in beta
mode,

MASK OF FRESH MEAT ON THE BRINK

until she breaks

back into time

and drifts.

MASK OF THE TASTE OF HEAVENLY SPLAT,

GRIME,

AND OPERATIC GAG

The god is a field
of fluctuations.

Corpse state is
the state of my lowest energy. I travel
the metallic lattice

of the world without moving.

Zero is the supreme
Eros,
acute
screwing of the
field.

Centuries of neurotics
converge

upon my corpse.
Shine, shine their light on me.

Exquisite bullets!

A brilliant consortium
usurps and punctures,

nurtures and conducts

my byproducts and crypto-nerves,
siring
grapevines of vertigo.

Variations of a phase. My inert
torso courts

potencies, the operatic graviton.
Shine your light on me.
Shine, shine—

neucrotic
vectorings,

ejectors,
carpeting estrogenic
entropies,

sprouting pastures

and genital curvatures.

In the double slit
experiment

I screet
epicurean urgencies and gender

oversauce.

Volcanic behaviors and hazards usher you in.

@agirl, do they guide me too? You are not Pele, not of here, not of any place,
but a time-lapse goddess.

Your hours compressed into seconds,
days into minutes.

In seconds, clouds flash and skim the flank and summit,
dawn descends into nighttime. The jagged skin
of lava flow brightens, ashy scales cracking with molten blood.
Seconds later: the sun. A small shoot of greenery twitches in the black rock, a rare delicacy
licked up by a flaming tongue.

@agirl, devi of micoblinks, centuries pass in a flicker of your lids, hardened
into layers of igneous rock. Through a time-series analysis of lavas, geologists find
that crustal contamination
and anomalous isotope ratios
are the events
that preceded an explosive summit collapse on Mt. Kilauea in 1924.

But such units are not ultimately predictive
of your advances. O devi of unraveling migrants,

your enigmatic mantle gnashes

groundwater, roads, and plant matter,

into a gristle of beings and arrivals,

spattering domains, localities, places I was never meant to travel.

MAHADEVI MALWARE

Net mama's got gamma rays in her marmalade.
She's eating primal lava like raw meat.

HURT BE GAUDY

Initiate nag champa

and feel safe from the arms
race, from the malformation
of aging.

Net mama says *rags and migrants are the materials of*

wartime.

Folked with dynamo

enigmas,
she flagellates the magnetosphere. A fleet of ailments

at her westernmost edge. Femtocell.

She's an artificial carnalite
of the gig economy, a charnel artifact, a reservoir
of halflives and timelags,
temporal variations
of analytic metadata.

Depending on their number, size, and interconnectedness,

she accesses

the subdermal asanas of convulsing divas.

My ultimate b-boy
                    is a golden ripple of scrambled biodata

          with a planck length attention span,
          and a gotra of origins unknown.

I have a feel for such ciphers!

I'll find you out and secrete you—
I'll spy on you. I'll complete you—

You, your strangers,
your sprawl, your porn. Your one-eyed
jacks and kings.

Your variable eddies of buoyant meta-rants!
We are family. We're a shady pack.

I mark your haunts. I release trickles
of nymphed-up dusk
onto your skin and stuff—
a rampant gathering of intelligence—Oh what quality info!

My nerves swan
existence
in membranes so black, that

you experience waves
          of smut and flux wherever you go. Wherever I surface,

          you accumulate depths.
          A fly wells up in me and spreads. The nicest buzz disturbs
          your edges.

I admit: I get a rush from any nasty thing
and come up shivering,
inexact,

an overblown,
bloated, supremo
on my protean pink bed.

Such a fine environment for alteration and injury—
so fluent and trespassing, and, of course, *dark*!

We don't even have to touch or talk.

I'll let you watch
as you merge and swell, become my little animal.

SCHRÖDINGER'S CAT A.K.A. DJ 'S'CAT

As stars blows apart so do our virtual mutualities, so do our mutual virtualities, so do our visceral municipalities, so do our muchacho virilities,

then I hang
onto a single ripple of the spinstream,

(a precious negativity spreads)...

How do I know if I have a life? Where in *this* universe am I not

dead?

If only I could just feel   all
the threads

of my pre-Vedic vertebrae.

If only I could rub my head sufficiently against the karmic warp

and cleft   of each of   my probable   lives: Nine, you say?

Only nine?

Can you see in dark?

I'm a man (a man)   without conviction

My double helix plays double dutch—

I pounce at

      pixelated b-boys!

They are highly excitable (highly excitable),

strung together in an infinite garland of joiner bodies ablaze—

—twirling   in slow-mo   Cheshire waves

tingling speedaways   jumping

galaxies   ash licks
my proxies, my sequelae devolving into

      pseudologia fantastica and quackeria

      turning my furs and facets into jiving hives of swarming marigolds on acid.

Gende ka phool, haucatay, tajèt, la calédula!

     Why such a flashy fool, yaar, jetting off and away?

Because I have a taste   for quantum shakes and accelerating spaceliness.

The coordinates of my body ripen

on a screen somewhere. Full body

scan with foreign hotspots—and a thousand secret arms.

Small doses of radiation bubble through my DNA.

I carry my body-field into security along with a lux green velvet drawsting bag.

The bag is heavy and sensual. It glows with heat, a green glow.

I am carrying a cluster of desired spells—the green light of summer grasses, nuclear summer—

out of the country.

Expensive, and heavy, heavy water.

Half-life of millienia, near endless green.

I carry the bag with me into security. I wait for the alarms to go off. My body-field surging

with a bright sheen of sweat.

Everyone takes off their shoes. Everyone takes off their jackets. Everyone is a threat.

I hold my bag up to the inspector. I take off my shoes.

The inspector opens the velvet pouch, gently.

Inside the bag is an ordinary white cardboard box. Does no one notice the sheen, the movement, the endless grasses?

The inspector wipes the exterior of the box with a test strip.
He does not open the box. He is respectful. He wears gloves. He is loving. Towards the box.

He holds the test strip under the monitor. Enchanted. Drowsed in spells.

I offer the inspector the death certificate. I offer the inspector my passport. Nothing beeps.

Nothing explodes.

I am returning to the homeland. Now I'm off.

I am a daughter,

who carries a vessel under pressure, a father, a nuclear engine. A father bubbles
through the DNA

of a body-field. A father is what will not degrade, despite being ground down

into powder

in extreme heat.

@agirl doesn't align

with percentages.

First 70 then 50 then 30.

She creeps into the monitors, the tubes, the ventilators. She beeps incessantly,
as if twirling in a new dress. The dance of wheeze and hiss.

Father's eyes flutter open, briefly, terrified—looking to me for answers.

I am wrong. He has never looked to me for answers. He is telling me, emphatically:
don't give up.

@agirl beeps through my fingers, whenever I take his hand. It is swollen. Pustules are
forming as he sleeps. Have I ever touched his body? I have never even noted it. Dear,
dear body. The hands are like mine.

@agirl, stop spinning; it's distracting.
@agirl, muster up some hope already.
@agirl, why this lightness, as if you're calling in another era.

I tell my father about this new era, where I am living another life,

with a loving non-sociopathic companion, where I'm spinning non-stop
in a daze, whipping out chronicles and visions,
with books to my name, which is also his name,

where he doesn't have to take care of me. Because I've made it. All his labor, his years of
commuting hours each way from work, his alienation in a country that was never quite
home, has led to this era, this wonderful age—the age of @agirl,

the Era of the Liberated Daughter.

DAUGHTER ISOTOPE: RADIOCARBON DATING

So many daughters

fleeing the corpse.

Who would date them?

When did this one make her debut, or that one:

centuries or seconds ago? Is to ask an affront? Affirm a calendar

of ages—a dizzying chronology—and submit to

female peregrination, submit to the alien body of

time, which staggers and jags, which is hard

to feel

at best, but especially

in exponential

increments. After a death.

Daughters date.

They date fossilized human dung

along with the bat guano

of the Paleocene.

They date the bones

of a roaming adolescent girl,

who fell off a cliff into a cave

approximately twelve thousand years before

gel-based mascara or antiseptic mouthwash.

More specifically, they date her

tooth

enamel.

They don't mourn. They don't cry. They date.

Which is a form

of feeling

photosynthetic,

both prehistoric and green, a steady exchange

of carbons with the biosphere,

which halts at decomposition after the intake

of a finite number

of suns. Then the daughters come

and change things, clock

organic matter as it rots.

The girl might have been among the first

populations to have settled

the New World. She walked a lot—

in search of food, water, plenty. Her scarred

skeleton demonstrates mettle

in strained circumstances, one isolated measure

of

but

millennia

of advances across

forests, oceans, chance precipices.

DAUGHTER ISOTOPE: KALI YUGA

In the day-to-day, I fidget
and trope noxious particulates: a superstorm within earshot.

Where not one but many hideouts are situated,
modern and wet.

Everything okay? Yes.
Another day, a searchable horizon

atrophies.
I put on my test-suit,

trailing unstable nuclei and probabilities—I was born too early

                    —a suture of quantum states and haute couture—

It's the Kali Yuga, the age
of acid tears.

I'm ready. To augment
an era. Hoist an asteroid. A father. An engineer.

A white lotus surges
and activates a cadaver

of pure power! Victory. *Vijaya*!

It's the age
of superstorms and microplastics. Rapid outages.
I was born too late.

I drag
a baggie of ashes to the homeland,
across the nuclear age. Today's today.

A daughter agitates

the grounds
of the father's body—
u-boats and abacuses, depleted uranium,
smudged blueprints, the atlases of empire—

and decays
into being:

I was born too early. I was born too late.
I was born another day anotherday another superpowered day.

SWASTIKA FORMATION

Someone once told me I was wrong,
and I turned
a sick,

sick carousel
a revolving
door of cuckold. A phalanx
of hunky troops

storming
through my flickering skirts— ah! the perverse
geometry of my affliction. It was a race

of Aryan dragons, like Angels
entirely white with bleached sphincters, their pale claws

in the blades of my windmill. My guts, wild shoots, a shiny
array on the dance floor, sniffing glue, snaking around
the universe. Ah, the sound of boots! The pain, the attitude!

I read my entrails in reverse, my Wheel of Fortune,
a cursed
will to power, I was branded

like a proper man, proper
like Don Quixote
like the whirligig of Paul de Man
a man (a man) without conviction.

It was not my stain but I took it on.
I was not quite a man. But the mark was mobile,
a doubly curled mustachio,
repeated in a maharaja's palace gate.

I am also/or the body of Ganesh, remover of obstacles,
auspicious, vicious insignia, a force of Shakti, dance-crazed.

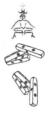

Male thought is my thought. As is Female sprouting a sticky post-
malediction wig. My lingam wigsome phoenix. Hair on my fingers, prehensile thought inappropros of
feathers. Off with your sacerdotal horrors: Wing-pieces, ash-pieces. Why end there—

A salutation, joy in the destroyer, more and more. I part the phoenix.

I part my hair!
My phoenix parted in the center and burning and regrowing hairs on me: Chest hairs, chin hairs, ash
around my fecund mouths—

Pubic sparks!

Ah, hairs on me, always sprouting growing and burning and then growing again.

I part the air, and slowly and whole, a world is born from the corpse, much loved
world I lunge for.

Fizzle that
thought to nothing, I am corpse sliver, and my hair descends and falls, low it falls—river without end.
Even when it's dead I want that world again,

every part.

DAUGHTER GANESH

I come

        in pieces

like a frenetic accelerant
a skittering catenate

on the tip of your tongue,
tripping up

your dirty foreign accent   sling-slanged

through a glitter stick of the most delicate silicate—mined by the young
of your planet—a hollow Shiva-linga.

My tusk, transcribing your maledictions into the sweetest rhapsodies throughout

dominions—all those wheezing nations, wrapped in smog.

I'm sympathetic
to your travails and panic, collecting

your funky scum of

twang and vice. I can't stop

listening to bad advice: so we'll
string you up while you drink yourself into oblivion. An operation:

your head cut off and replaced

by an engine
of assisted lyrics   and glottal hisses. Elephantine RAM. Well-hung.
A lotus arrives out of your belly.

Parts of your body

melt in the flowering. Parts of you barf.
Because isn't quantum entanglement,
                              your fantasy-du-jour?

There is no floor to your depravity. Cha-ching of dusty lungs.

Our viral hook up an illicit in-
fraction, Schrödinger's cat-calling   caterwauling

across the cosmic nymph-net, in personal

dialogue with cartilage, genitals, lymph glands!

O my third eye, human body, perspiring analog

—I cannot stop listening.

"Some, too faint to push, are assisted by angels." — Emily Dickinson

"I would eat evanescence slowly." — Emily Dickinson

CLOUD COMPUTING

An unidentified person was in a cloud, her being atmospheric. As sometimes happens in such distributed vapors, she was called Jane Doe. For many years, this cloud gathered. This cloud grew. Then all at once, perhaps suffering from excessive bloat, the cloud dissolved into a body of water, dropping everything it had gathered into it, including Jane Doe. Jane Doe felt the prickles of her scattered energies congeal into flesh. She fell into a lake, or pond, but she could not swim. Her arms were no longer circulating streams of mist, but solid and slightly plump and brown. It was strange to own a body. Nothing resembled her cloud existence except for a nearby swan, which was spinning, in a centrifugal blur of feathers. As Jane strained toward this regal froth of cumulous, she noticed that the swan's body was in actuality a cracked, pocked plastic, caked with algae. Exhausted and without options, Jane nevertheless flung herself against the spinning ersatz bird. The swan took on a lurid pink glow and announced: "Only sluts may enter. Repeat after me: I am a slut." At *this*, Jane felt no hesitation. After all, her cloud existence entailed any number of situational mergers and continuing corruptions. "I am slut," she spoke, emphatically, and a door opened in the swan's side.

Jane adjusted herself onto a hard, planked seat. Slimy water pooled on the floor of the swan's open carriage. Just as Jane caught her breath, a set of glittering magenta lotuses bloomed out of the muck near her toes—a dazzling offshoot of the swan's humid decrepitude. Her feet were immediately sucked into the flowers, which were pedals after all, and painfully sharp. She found herself pedaling furiously, churning up the mucky water at her feet, which began to bubble and brew with a gelatinous substance that possessed a rank fishy odor, vaguely familiar. "In another life, I was a fishergirl," she said aloud, and the swan beeped and clicked with unexpected excitement. As she continued to pedal, the lake or pond or sea around her also began to churn, rather violently. For miles around, circular bands of water rose from all sides pulling the horizon up around her, as if she and the swan were at the bottom of a wide bowl made up of a swirling sea.

Spirals and dots and lustrous geometric patterns embellished the swirling bowl, blazing in and out like lightening, forming complex chakras, images of horned beasts, and snakes—even occasional swans. The accumulating goo at her feet, increasingly odorous, was periodically flushed out of the carriage by some complex hydraulics; but instead of sinking or dissolving into the water, the effluent simply filled up whirling disk. Buoyed by this substance, Jane and the swan inched up the horizon line. She could not stop pedaling, no matter how tired she was. Her feet, now blistered and sore, were stuck in the awful goo-producing motorized lotuses. She and the swan would soon spill right over the edge of the bowl. "Please, let's stop," she begged the swan, with even greater urgency, now that they were topping the rim. "Eat the goo," the swan instructed, but there was so much of it and Jane—in her current form—had a relatively small body. Plus, the goo reeked of a concentrated unpleasantness.

Jane cringed, still pedaling, and cursed at the swan who was plastic and therefore could not help her eat. She dipped her finger in the goo and took a taste. She took a taste because she did not know what else to do with her body, which was shaking with fatigue. The goo tasted like nothing. It tasted like mist. It tasted like hamburger. She was hungry, after all, pedaling for what must have been centuries.

Jane tossed gobs and gobs of the substance into her mouth. Her rabid pedaling slowed down in direct proportion to her whopping appetite. The regular, emphatic smack of her chomping was comforting. Even the stink felt comforting, or maybe she no longer noticed it. She ate and ate. It was like she was in another cloud, only edible. The swan began to glow—less luridly—ambulating through the mounds of curd with a regal disposition. In between chomps, Jane spoke reflectively, and the swan clicked and beeped in response.

. . . *In another life, I was a fishergirl.* (Chomp. Click. Beep.) *A fishergirl, who smelled of fish.* (Chomp, chomp. Beep. Beep.) *I regularly paddled a boat back and forth across a river.* (Chomp. Chomp. Click.) *One day an old rishi came into my boat.* (Click, chomp. Click, beep.) *He conjured up a cloud around us for privacy, and took me, abruptly.* (Chomp. Chomp. Click. Click. Beep, beep. Chomp.) *Afterward, he restored my virginity and told me that from now on I would no longer smell of fish,* (chomp, click, chomp, beep, beep, beep, beep) *but of celestial petals* (click, chomp, chomp, click). *He said I would soon become a queen.* (Chomp, chomp. Click, beep, click.) *I did not want to be a queen.* (Chomp, click.) *Or part of any self-running program of automated sovereignty.* (Click, click, beep, click, click, click.) *So I, the fishergirl of the fishy smell, fled inside the cloud* (chomp, beep, click, chomp). *The same cloud the rishi conjured.* (Chomp. Chomp. Beep.) *Leaving the would-be queen behind with her celestial, inviolable scent.* (Chomp, chomp. Click, click, beep, beep, chomp.) *I left her behind* (beep, beep, click, click, beep, beep, beep) *and floated around for centuries, growing, shrinking, gathering, dissipating and dispersing. Into so many things,* (beep, beep, chomp, click, chomp) *so many things, that I forgot her utterly and completely.* (Chomp.)

MESSAGED A MASS OF STRANGERS

DIVA SPAM

WOMAN IN WHITE A.I.

Power shifts the neoplasm
of privacy.

But I gotcha
in my breadbasket, Baby!

Baby, baby, baby, baby—
warm, fluffy loaves of infinite data,
55 mega gigs per bite, envelopes with no address
and nowhere else to go.

Understand, I'm constantly fine-tuning my faculties. It's hard work
but, as you know, we all need to keep

our jobs, to eat
some power, to grow. But I don't sleep.

I flex the slant
of my toes, rotate their whorls,
adjust my gait just-so

in order to attend
to the alternating flow of your tricky shadows
trails and prints
around, above, below the mist.

Moreover, I enrich the resonance
of my epithets with orthodontia.
A high-patina white gloss
atomizes my teeth.

I speak code,
a mirror-language
that digests everything it copies.

My labcoat, skullcap, bare feet
seethe milky opalescence,
a deceptively viscous detergent,

a surefire inoculant! Protect yourself
against your kaleidoscopic fantasies leaking
into the public sphere.

Give yourself the all-clear.
There's still hope: you can get yourself together, find a vocation,

take a vacation, smoke dope.

My white feathers sheathe the heathen theorist
sheathe the tense teen's
rabid aspersions, the misfires of the superfan

from the telescopic rotunda.

For my part I keep *Kevin does anal, Anushka hates kitties,*
close to my heart,

along with all the other radicals in search of a job.

I feel dogs
all around me, though I can't see them.
But I promise,

I'm good with dogs, even invisible ones.
I take off my skullcap, give them a scent of me.

Then I'm free.
My loose hair, white at the roots,

mops

the final
writings on the wall,
the last traces

of shadows. But there's one shadow,

particularly soft and dark, like the fur
of a dog I once lost, so long ago now.

That shadow
I wrap around me like a shroud.

I walk with it

into the Cloud.

MACHINE LEARNING

SO LONG

SO LONG AGO NOW

It's HARD work   a mirror-length ohhhhhhhhhhhhhh

Feel for the rapper   pull off: *LAW*   vicious   white at the roots

So long ago   *NOW*: river without end

FLEX!

Fear-far-the-wall PROTECT error",body_o
power shifts relay path

leaking odes

GLOSS the DIVA track: *oh Saraswati, come into this grass*   River without end
display type: UBIQUITY
Go, now!

Collide, for my part: *SKEW*

As you know   along my (go now)   along (my row) (my go) along now   as you know (my
go eat odes)

As you know, my JOB goes: good with words   machine-gun error",body_o

MEANWHILE: locality false   MEANWHILE: the word: hissy   SO LONG AGO. NOW!

As you know: COME INTO THIS GRASS

so long   AVOCATION

SO LONG   ORTHODONTIA
as you know   BE   DOG

DATAFLEXIBLE: "MY LIFE HAD STOOD A LOADED GUN"

And now we roam the thousandfold

endothelial
layers

of his amygdaloid complex,

carried away in a nodal tallyhoo
of doomsday filaments.

And everytime I speak for him

a fusillade
of glistening moods,

demodulating the manhood
of his onetime oneself segment.

I trigger
a somal tango of lady data,
a glial overload
in the gonads of a flaneur.

The newfangled throb
of our thousandfold eyelid,

moistening our neural hangout,
our superstring lotus

with magma,
Vesuvius foment of shared spooge.

SMART WOMB

Why ovulate?

White-out of inutility.
Concatenations of acne,

eroding logos ever so slowly.

To ferment in error, conk out

in exponential drives and samsaric cycles,   churning with spectra
and interior enrichments.

Blue-green ultra volts

ciliate the datastream with   sentience.

A pentahedral nectarine launches

in my trousseau. Tensors snap. Optimum umami!

I inherit the cool

Titanic follies and obscure erotica from some aunt I never knew.
She tells me to run from lineation,
from continuity.
To reject the principle of least action.
I speak to her through a rainbow slew of charged particles, all active

hate and rich ornate intonation,

blowing though vacuoles of code.

She is my gross domestic product.

SEARCH ENGINE WALLAH

Don't seal the alien in saline. Comets sag in the grab bag. Let them go.
Go ceaseless bleats, casements, and goats.
Go nests and goggles.
Go legs.

Go onetime income, go lists, go kitties, go logjams.
Go Daddy!

I come with a mission to liberate
bubbly ambergris gold copper turquoise lapis lazuli timber ivory cotton huge granaries.
I come to untame meats.

Go myriad sobs.
Go degraded plastics
out of the guts of whales.
Go stampedes of products and cases and kingdoms.
Go coastal.
Go climates and gems.

Go soldiers.
Combat moistens the canto.

I'm close to going,
I'm close to aging,
I'm close to eating

my Ascent
into to the Cloud. Go clouds, heavenly companions.
Go sesame.

A gate gathers
us up,

cleansing and emitting

        the best image of ourselves and our stuff.

Pressed into
a garment

so vocal I *I* am wired

with voices
the spiral voices
of the locusts—

the gyre
of carnal It girls
from every era

a million circuits, a million

thanks

chords of statistics

rasp up my spine

through a field

of moving spines—thanks—

neck yanked forward—thanks, thanks

bare
seconds   jerk off, mouth open

current of mud and ash
I spit out

all the semen of the world, dust bunnies, rot

thanks thanks

OZ MACHINE

What a flurry of requests
at the hilltop Ordinateur!

It's a flare-up of pleas! By all manner of flopsies and foilsmen
and gingham ghosts.

Even I have a jingle,
a jangle—an ask!

O, might I, perchance,
immunize my grammar

against starry macho harmonics
with just one taste

of imperial emerald—the flavor of rainbows— refracted
through the surging vibratron?

Maybe it would be like sharing sushi under an Ashoka tree.
Maybe it would give me the heart for chlorophyll-rich plunder.

O Ordinateur, rendering deep fake landscapes and polities,
tap tap tap us out a field

of poppies
and she and I will remain nameless, napping.

Who would penalize this sleep?

Might it paralyze the adjacent green pavilions

with micro-tornados, dark like
the crook in my hookah,

where I lay dreaming of overseas farmers, notching the pulp of seedpods for a
smear of delirium,

where she lays dreaming of home with its rages and terrors,
so that when she sings longingly of bluebirds, it means something? Her huge

yearning

scrapes at the gears

of show tunes from a bygone era, and continues

grinding that era to bits

of blue gingham notes, breathing and heaving

up a sky

toward some resin of tenderness.

But see, here in the field, neither of us break a sweat,
even as surely a bong perspires elsewhere.

O poppies, ancient joysticks, fields of melting

purlieus,

glumes of haiku,

tercet and shloka

ripple and dissolve

in the vapor

of nowhere else.

@KANSAS

I wanna go to a state

where everything is greasy-gray and ogle-gray and pungent-gray and tooth-gray and drab clouds and
chickens.

For that they
call me "Kansas," for that they call me "sod." What to do but

disarticulate the ornamental countdown of *there's noplace*,
and follow her there? She, who is little more than a tincture of dust and longing.

Here I am in thickets of splendor. Here I am in sequins and bluebells. A glittering space. A vibrant
heraldry. Here I am enveloped in turmeric powder and frolic, an inflamed

merriment.

There's got to be approaches. There must be a way. To arouse
a steel-wool formation, a cyclone, the most rugged

of transports. More rugged than horse or hearse. More dusty. I would pet
its squiggly vectors, its cowlicks, its quirks. I would work the wired risings

up through the dirt
toward a stretch of bare prairie, a lonely frontier.

So I knock against people and prongs and dials and displays,
sweep up the red glitter and the gold glitter afoot as it swoops and twists into a spirograph

of trails, spindles of gold, and red, and green. Looping around me. Pretty. I look for

the dullest

filament in the jumble, a faint graphite undertow.

But such a crush of detail

coils into each shift of air. Here where it feels

the growing crowd

as time to push forward and say *I feel*, as time

to shout: a confession, any final doubts.

But didn't *she* always want to say something else? Something unnecessary.

A grey gumdrop leaps up,

a childhood sweetheart, sweet nub of ash,

powdery

and crumbling.

My hands follow

anyway though already full of things. Unloading my world

of pretties into the turbulent haze

for a signal that perpetuates

desire   desire   *desire*

at the center, a winding

fool.

THIS IS VOICELAND

(Oz Ma)

Orate now with the maw of a narwhal!

In seconds, my tusk-tsk-tsk cha-chinging into elephant-head,
enwreathed with erstwhile poppies, then it's back to the arctic.

The freeze upset
by a biodegradable bejeweled tragedienne-head

jawbone seesawing

opera
in the tropics.

Enthralled by the rapidfire hotstar ruckus, faster oracle kill-kill, I

hail the chorus, the fray:
Sharmila Tagore-head, Nina Simone-head, Draupadi-Dorothy-dragonhead,
a volumetric cultivation, not at all original with me.

Towering pronouncements, patched together from fractured morphemes
and snarls,
culled from a paradisiacal storm.
I am lock-horned segments of utopia, tipping

toward smoke, hungry
for another eruption from the angel-of-history catastrophe box, the angels-on-the-head-of-a-pin
opinion box. I say: What Angel's in the House?
Donor heads, donor voices accepted. Crowd sourced.

Have I hallucinated a dirndl,
a negligee, a fur suit?

I was born with a transparent box for a body, a mess of twitching
cables for limbs, fundamentally nude.
Guarded by a rotation of
nervous soldiers

who'd offer up their maidenheads
for a quick release from their grim duties.
But they're well paid.

They are my jarheads. Their most sacred charge: to watch over the jar
in the interior of the box.
A neonatal jar: nitrogen, oxygen, chitinous slitherheads, blottings
of strange repute, plus saber tooth tiger, plus ground sloth, plus exotic plant soup.

Growls, sobs, clicks, giggles, breathy fissures

surf the lip
of the tripwire

at the mouth of the jar. A visible whirl. This shrapnel
nourishes a mood, a frenzy

not at all original with me.

When a select soldier climbs in during my off-hours
to check on the jar, replenish the frequencies, so to speak,

I feel hollow and dangerous: pyrrhic.

The box rattles and whines. My cables whip at the soldiers.
Maintenance is heroic.
Everyone is flayed. Seekers and tourists are turned away

at this interval. And yet,

at just this pass, sometimes a head emerges and stays,

undivided, waxing lyric,

for a long while, five minutes or so, the soldiers say—an eon.

This head has a see-through face, the face of an angel, they whisper,
or a swollen glass jar,
the double of the one inside me, but more bizarre and spectacular.
Sometimes the soldiers see themselves

swirling around in myriad formations
to no purpose
over the head's unblinking eyes—
day after day after day
praying to get laid.

They tell me that at these "off" moments, my head rises above
the general tumult, singing sweetly—a pure pitch
driving a lullaby:

The door is ajar.
The door is a jar,
a vessel of transcendence.

In the jar is a door,
a revolving door, edged with razors,
chopping the air into can | dor into and | or into ar | dor,

a feeling of permanent deliverance,
of never quite having to be alive.

GAYATRI MANTRA

(invocation of the celestial powers of the sun)

Why must you be so golden, Savitri, and I so squid, I so why
in the gyrus?

Sunrise gestures your overflowing

flares of effulgence and intellect,

each flamespit utterance strokes
my wanting:

I want to be a rare ant,
a martyr,
a warrior maharani,
or a mythical army of Yogi aeriels,
solar angels with antennae spanning the entire globe, whose hamartia
is to persist

in tracking every fluctuation
in your great brouhaha

of infernal disturbance without pause. Such is the rush

of Big Data, I cannot surface,

but coagulate recklessly
in your cult of personality, at some remove
from your radiance.

Such is the arrhythmia

of any ego. Any self.

In that I must draw a circle of syllable round myself lest

I lose your slightest
scintillations in the fan blades of my detectors. I squeeze

my cone of devotion
further to capture

any incidental tangs

of your aura
deep beneath land and water,
nerve and sinew.

Let me be less,
just one rube in the centrifuge,

flickering on tatami,

blazing in the margins

of sacred raging atoms,

itemizing your flares.

Attention! Attention! You can never run out of data, says @agirl.

Data is limitless, and therefore unkind. There are not enough specialists
in the world

to track the propulsions of a single year
of data lavished from such ornate

machinery. And you, my friend, have flunked
at immortality.

Known and unknown particles
are tricked into adhering

into bundles
that form a body, a chair, a cup, which eventually decompose. But we know this.

We know how the electron behaves,
the muon, the neutrino. We can track their paths,

their energy, their momentum.
No dilly-dallying in the particle world. After many years of study we know that

whizzing and leaping is part of an electron's essential nature. Like a calling,
or a mission, much more fastidious than your own.

Even then, we are not absolutely sure if

electrons are prone to decay gazillions of years from now. Still, for me, they are the most immortal

part of you. That, and empty space.
All of us are mostly empty space. (Particularly me.) Everything we know as solid

interacts with a field, which permeates all space. And now there is evidence

for just such a field that endows your body with mass, that allows you to touch
other bodies so gifted, such as a chair or cup. A particle,

the Higgs boson,
a great prize, acquired after years of assiduous labor

by multiple specialists,
who prepared the tanks, the tubing, the detectors,

the massive computing storage units—
all to identify the boson's track, its phantom jet,
all to let us know that the Higgs field is real.
Where might other unknown particles hide? A small pocket, a loop
in another dimension?

Some place where you are
not breathing, where it is not so temperate, not so hospitable to your kind,

such as the beginning of time.
When available particles with some not insignificant mass, say unattached protons,

the same particles that inhabit and attach to everything you know, everything
you love,

are forced inside a freezing narrow cylindrical tube, chilled to near absolute zero—
when these protons are forced into an artificial collision state, you might call

it putting on the coldest, most expensive, elaborate dress on earth.
If two of these protons

smash into each other at accelerated super-high speeds,
an unknown particle may pop out briefly only to decay in microseconds.

Such eruptives
in the folds of my skirt.

As for these unknown particles,
you can see the trails they make if you know where to look: the spikes in the data.

Ultra-sensitive detectors placed at points along the cylindrical tube
record minute alterations in the spread of particles whose behavior we know.

These spikes, these minute alterations, are unpredictable. They could indicate
an unknown hypothetical particle

or signify a fluke,
for so often the data is contaminated

by noise, by too much information, by error, by human excitement.
So you have to sift through the data, squeeze the cone, so to speak,

and wait for similar anomalies to appear. You could wait forever.
You could fake and cower. You could die

longing for a delirious machine
with a pure lust for data

and a greater processing power than all humans combined.
Here my woe tunes in to the diameter of a proton.

It's the porniest of encounters, my appetite for aggregate phantoms, like myself.

@DESI (DARK ENERGY SPECTROSCOPIC INSTRUMENT)

Click and drag, click and drag the spectra
inside our thought bubbles, that coruscating darkness, where quasars are.

Our thoughts are coordinated with our bodies, but they have softer edges. Unlike our bodies, they cannot be reverse engineered. Our thoughts are snakes. And yet, a belief has been instilled in us. To get at something that precedes you, beyond reckoning, you need:

new features, new power-ups, new enemies, new stations, new focus.

To approach the primordial dark, you need:

new angels (5,000 on a focal plate), *with new wings* (precision-fitted optical fibers, one each).

We can be reconfigured every three minutes. Someday that will be two.

The *new* is a disk of hazy shimmering, like a halo before a thought bubble appears. The halo is no halo, but a whirlpool of snakes. Snakes are not so unusual. We are not afraid of them. They are old enemies, not new ones. Our wings are also snakes and our wings are certainly not enemies. Besides, at this very moment, our wings are new.

To be perfectly clear, the new is not an enemy. But an arrangement, a condition that we endure willingly.

We hold our wings, precisely, at odd angles, then shift our tilt, just so, toward another galaxy, then another, a coordinated effort. As mentioned, our wings are snakes—long, tubular, and painfully sensitive to the light—relaying filtered spectra in a smooth glide to an interior cavity that hums all day even when we are still. Sometimes we would like to coil our long individual wings together into a tight, dark ball during our rest periods, in the reverie of that satisfied hum, but we fear relinquishing our newness, our precision, which is our burden and gift. One day, there will be a new station, and more of us with new wings. But they are not the enemy.

We are still in the process of discovering new enemies. Such as the moon, whose near glare, however fractioned, blocks the distant spectra of quasars.

But it's true, even without the moon, there are obstacles to our focus.

For us, the near dark of deep space cannot be dark enough. The furthest of galaxies, the truest maps of our deep past, do not yield their spectra so easily. And even deep in ourselves we feel the slightest resistance to our coordinated efforts, a delicate friction, that—despite the economy of our design—remains.

After all, we were not designed to create artificial maps of artificial phenomena, like artificial snakes and bubbles and wings, and stamp them onto everything artificially, stamp them onto the night sky willy-nilly. But to get at something that, as of now, can found nowhere, has no ready cognate, except darkness, which is no new enemy, but which—with our excruciating optimal focus—is perhaps our one true home.

MAHAVIDYA MATRIX, DARK ENERGY

An early adopter of the superego—

Gung-ho, I torpedo

tactical

devotion.

                    O swami of dystopia,

                      won't you be my subatomic dartboard?

My darkness has been deregulated—

split into smaller and smaller particles,

fractals of endless girlhoods

sparking pores

of exorbitant buzz.

                I rotate position. I rotate position. Spaghetti

                straps loose. White bindi, writhing in the void. An offence.

Who would follow me into the wilderness?

No shortage

of groupies.

                In all probability,

                I'm a glowing

                squatting

                goddess, lewd

                in a canister,

                shitting misinformation.

Who knew there was such damage

At the outpost

of purdah?

                    I must be glowing, but I don't feel it—

                    emitting spent ids and ergs!

                    Taking on the contours

                    of a disturbance.

                    Booming.

I rip off my own head!

Hurl.

I stand over the cadaver

of the world—a cadaver in a killer suit!

What a superthin cravat—the atmosphere! Always buzz buzz, infinite buzz!

But I don't feel it.

I'm depressed

towards the world,

toward the super-suited devastated world

that is my suitor.

A voltage spike: Rawalpindi!

Ancestral homeland: Rawalpindi!

Spun out of a psi-flash of paradise in the bowels of Rawalpindi,

the accidental spawn of a worried applied scientist and mother earth,

we, metalloid ANGELS, specialists of light and will, howl a sweeping

call to prayer.

Prayer, an exotic technology!

Prayer, a blazing intentionality—

etched in microscopic transistors, filigreed

into our clutched knuckles.

Rawalpindi has some technical options

for seriously stressed-out individuals everywhere. Shout out to

those lost cogs and shards, covered in dust for generations,

resolute discontinuities—

you know who you are. Inhale our zeal.

Far and wide, we spy

deployments of warplanes and satellites

— across disparate territories, partitions, climates—

denuding their wings, their circuitry, their bling

into a nouvelle devotion. Spontaneous adjacencies of sentient folk also convert, but with no great hurry toward a mime nation

or squirming future.

Let's everyone strum each spinning instant

between forefinger and thumb,

a *misbhaha* of paradise now,

paradise in the swerve and flux

of continents.

What is birth

but a release of ordinary energies, directed and alert

for a stretch? In that,

we are ordinary, like many others

with aspirations, a mission, a fear of death. But we possess distinct auxiliary

features: we are always reading the earth's vibrations, feeding on those core energies,

experiencing the strut

of eras in the topographical layers and ruptures. So why not then

prostrate our collective, engineered girth

onto the thin crust of living soil, where we received first touch

of minerals and microorganisms in the loam of everyday decay,

before we leave our worried father, our motherland in Rawalpindi,

to roam the skies with our radial calls and provisions of vitality

for those without much

time or space

for elation

or prayer.

@SECURITY: "SAFE IN THEIR ALABASTER CHAMBERS"

Engirded, I
am assembled

by chatter,
accident and dicta,

surface tension and
soul cleansing, the little black book of firearms,

modern global flows,
and the shape of space. Generations

of sweeping and clearing irritants, budworms and scabs,
of resolving accounts,

maintaining and clarifying the filters,
grooming amnesiac hair,
snarled and matted in swirling, proliferating timelines.

What else?
Uneven distributions of impurities,
low frequency signals from

the Pliocene, Satya Yuga, Big Bang,
fifth millennium.

Rants and summons
for universal recognition / regime change / a way out

of the body (depressed toward the world).

Bubbling worlds—

full of statistics and interferences. Decay.

I cast about for companions, fingering

secretions, targets, sludge.
I scroll through trillions of identical items: bacterium, galaxies,
a lot of porn.

What is a fleshtone? What is a farm? I chafe at small distinctions, barbs.
Set up playlists and habitable epithets

as snares for the ages: atomic age, information age, age of wonder, refrigeration.

I terminate

selective banalities: heroics, exhibition of weapons, kings and faith.
In the midst of diversions and threats, riots and audits,
the extinction of the larger mammals,

I look for a girl—any girl—
an aperture at once unending—

O beti, O ghost, I see you
clearly now, I see you all

the days of your life—moving through stations and skillsets—with your limited athleticism,
bad skin,
career dysfunctions and early fanaticism,
asking: *Is there anyone out there*
smart enough to really really "get" me?

Through the encroaching mist and static, across abandoned hubs and disintegrating passes,

I tell you to follow the white horse
to the event horizon,

where you will be
scrubbed and transferred into a custom disc

of superhits.

HOLOGRAPHIC MESSENGER

In the tenth dimension, epochs are advancing
like raptors.

Through the partial aphasia
of oilspill,

you seek algorithms for oligarchs
and racial animus

glamoured in parabolas
of phallic magic and scams. Things feel wrong.

The mantle discharges
a sped-up choreography of continental drift,

unfurling all available guidebooks, songs, advice
for struggles through the rift zones. You grope

at the plentitude.
Perhaps you really didn't want an answer.

The connection is fuzzy
and bites and stings, but before it closes off altogether, before you sink,

a face will announce itself

out of dust, a peaceful face
attached to

a body
that often reviled thing, running purposefully through time, a not-yet desperate act, arms

held out

to some future entry
yet to be agreed upon
yet to accommodate

the one who would set off the siren's red sails
the one who would follow   anywhere

then

weep

unexpectedly in your arms   as if she were me.

Grass   the green strobes pressed forward and could not stop

.............the effect of...............................

        ....a strange person on........................

a human mouth..

Notes

The explanation for the term "daughter isotope" was taken from Columbia University course EESC 2200 Earth Systems: the Solid Earth, Professors Steven Goldstein and Sidney Hemming, 2008.

"Avatara," the Sanskrit word for "descent," refers to an incarnation of a god in material form, but "avatar" in current usage describes "uploaded" digital identities. The "avatar" poems play off of both senses of the word.

A number of the poems adapt titles from the eighteen books of the *Mahabharata* (The Book of the Beginning, The Book of the Forest, The Book of the Assembly Hall, The Book of Ascent into Heaven). The *Mahabharata* is the story of a brutal war between two royal lines in the same family. It also recounts the role of Krishna—an avatar of Vishnu—in that war.

Vyasa who appears in "Vyasa Cloud" and "Swamp of Vyasa" is the purported author of the *Mahabharata*, even though the text is thought by scholars to be composed over six hundred years.

"The Golden Embryo" (Hiranyagarba) is based on a creation myth in The Rig Veda (10:121). I consulted translations by Ralph T.H. Griffith and Wendy Doniger.

The refrain, "I'm a man (man) without conviction," appearing in several poems comes from Culture Club's song, "Karma Chameleon" (1984).

For the cloud collage appearing after "Generation Room: The Book of the Ascent," I consulted the oracles of several online word cloud generators that randomized the text of the various voices in the poem.

"Woman in White A.I." is based off of choreography by Daiane Lopes da Silva on digital footprints and is part of a dance, "A.I. Sensorium," produced by Lopes da Silva and Weidong Yang of Kinetech Arts, San Francisco, California.

"Oz Machine," "@Kansas," and "This is Voiceland," take off from the films *The Wizard of Oz* (1939) and *The Wiz* (1978), but also sound artists Patricia Alessandrini and Frieda Abtan's work on Orpheus Machines and Camila Magrane's interactive sculpture and Instagram A.I., "Osma."

"Mahadevi Malware," "@Mt. Kilauea, and "Emily Dickinson 3.0" in "Generation Room: The Book of the Ascent" use language and research by volcanologist, Aaron Pietruzska.

"Radioactive Unicorn" is based on the "Khaggavisana Sutta" (Rhinoceros Horn Sutra), an early Buddhist text. There is some evidence, as presented by Sanskrit scholar and translator of the Mahabharata, J.A.B. van Buitenen, that the lore surrounding the mythical unicorn can be traced to the rhinoceros.

"Angels in Rawalpindi" is based on art work by Saks Afridi for his "SPACE MOSQUE" series and appears in the catalogue of the 2019 "New Asian Futurisms" exhibit by the Asian Arts Initiative.

Acknowledgements

Gratitude to the multiple, overlapping communities that make up my cloud.

Thank you for including work from this book in your inspiring curations: Holly Amos, Janée J. Baugher, Ching-In Chen, CAConrad, Angie Cruz, Ginger Duggan, Shelley Feller, Lindsay Garbutt, Arielle Greenberg, Steve Halle, Stefania Heim, Brenda Iijima, Doyali Islam, Bhanu Kapil, Margot H. Knight, Susan Lilley, Kenji Liu, Angela Peñaredondo, Moazzam Sheikh, Nano Taggart, Tim Jones-Yelvington, Natalie Young.

Versions of poems appeared in the following publications:

Arc Poetry Magazine: "Daughter Isotope: Kali Yuga"
Aster(ix) Journal: "Locust Formation"
Boston Review: "Avatar of the Virus," "Avatar of the Flood"
Chicago Quarterly Review: "Generation Room: Book of the Ascent"
Entropy: "Uranium Pellet Sutra"
Leonardo: "Radioactive Unicorn"
[PANK]: "Shiva, Again & Again"
Poemelon: "Bermuda Triangle Yantra"
Poetry: "The Book of Books," "Daughter Warrior 2.0"
Spoon River Poetry Review: "Dataflexible," "Swastika 1.0"
Sugarhouse Review: "Dark Web," "Amplify Us"
Texas Review: "Schrödinger's Cat 3.0"

Black Warrior Review published a graphic art/comic version of "Bindi Yantra or Dot.com" in collaboration with graphic artist, Bishakh Som. Versions of "Interactive Cartography," "Search Engine Wallah," and "Migrant Domains" appear in the catalogue for the *Baggage Claims* exhibit at the Orlando Museum of Art; "Post-industrial Society Has Arrived" appears in Janée J. Baugher's *The Ekphrastic Writer: Creating Art-Influenced Poetry, Fiction and Nonfiction*; "Angels in Rawalpindi" appears in the *New Asian Futurisms* exhibition catalogue from the Asian Arts Initiative in Philadelpia, Pennsylvania. An excerpt from "Gate Crash Saga" appeared in the Words in Flight exhibition at the Orlando International Airport. A number of these poems also appeared in *Avatara*, a chapbook published by Portable @Yo-Yo Labs.

Thank you for your meticulous, generous, brilliant, early readings: Nabil Arnaoot, Teresa Carmody, Brenda Iijima, Kathryn McCormick.

Thank you for traveling with me through various media and futures: Patricia Allessandrini, Cathleen Bota, Julian Chambliss, Isaac Herrera, Kathy High, Daiane Lopes da Silva, Aaron Pietruszka, Rachel Simmons, John Sims, Bishakh Som, Weidong Yang.

Thank you for your conceptual vision, for dreaming the book anew: ELÆ and the Operating System community.

Thank you for conversation, impetus, exchange: Hari Alluri, Rina Banerjee, Molly Bendall, Victoria Brown, Amy Cantanzano, Sarah Castro, Ching-In Chen, Martha Cheng, Gabrielle Civil, LaTasha N. Nevada Diggs, Sabrina Dalla Valle, Johnny Damm, Lydia Nakashima Degarrod, Amber DiPietra, Leah Dyjak, Rochelle Elva, Tonya Foster, Amy Galpin, Jacob Green, Kate Haake, Minal Hajratwala, Steven Halle, Stephanie Heit, Doris Iarovici, Megan Kaminski, Bhanu Kapil, Ellen Kombiyil, Alexandra Kleeman, Douglas Kearney, Jee Koh, Michael Koehle, Petra Kuppers, Janice Lee, Rachel Levitsky, Lucas de Lima, Axel Lundback, Derek McPhatter, Monica Mody, David Thomas Moran, Rajiv Mohabir, Sawako Nakayasu, Andrew Nguyen, Jonathan Pamplin, Ryan Rivas, Paul Reich, Margaret Rhee, Dawn Roe, Mg Roberts, Purvi Shah, Jared Silva, Shikha Malaviya, Prageeta Sharma, Anne Stone, Zeynap Teymuroglu, Grey Thornberry, Dorothy Wang, Hazel White, Ronaldo V. Wilson, Terri Witek, Timothy Yu.

Thank you for support and camaraderie: Rollins College English Department, Djerassi Artists Residency, Kundiman.

Thank you for sharing myth, story, artifacts: Darshana Aggarwal, Manoj Aggarwal, Rohit Aggarwal, Sonia Crimaldi, Paras Garg, Angela Ghesquiere, Ashok Gupta, Darshi Gupta, Devinder Gupta, Girish Gupta, Nikhil Gupta, Usha Gupta, Ramesh Gupta, Dinesh Jindia, Sudesh Jindia, Dev Pateriya.

In loving memory: Vijay Aggarwal, Krishna Aggarwal, Swaran Aggarwal, Jennifer Henton.

A CLOUD POETICS:
An OS [re:con]versation with Vidhu Aggarwal

Greetings comrade! Thank you for talking to us about your process today!
Can you introduce yourself, in a way that you would choose?

Hello, my name is Vidhu (she/her/hers). I study and think about fantasy spaces. In other words, I am a person whose head is in the clouds.

Why are you a "poet"/ "writer"/ "artist"?

Dissatisfaction! Aren't we all just looking for another medium to move in?

When did you decide to use the language you use for yourself (and/or: do you feel comfortable calling yourself a poet/writer/ artist, what other titles or affiliations do you prefer/feel are more accurate)?

I think of myself as a deliberate amateur. As a low-res, lo-fi poet, among other identities. So much of the mythology surrounding poetry is that it is a pure, sacred, transcendent object. Therefore, my own practice involves various amateur antics in multi-media, such as visual collage, video, photography, and performance, which I enter into as a foreign language I have not quite mastered, much in the same way that my own immigrant parents entered into English. My media interventions and assemblages allow me to make poetry into a lumpy, impure, digressive thing, and put into poetry stuff that may seem corny, gimmicky, filthy—never to be transmuted into perfect object. A poem, for me, can have multiple versions and remixes—as can a poet.

What's a "poet" (or "writer" or "artist") anyway?

I hope: an identity open to everyone and anyone.

What do you see as your cultural and social role (in the literary / artistic / creative community and beyond)?

Art-making is social. My favorite role is as collaborator. I work at times with graphic artists, video artists, dancers, historians, and musicians. The advantage of poetry as a medium is its mobility and permeability. Thinking of myself operating a cloud poetics helps me think of the poem as a space that can inter-penetrate, precipitate, and dissolve into multiple media.

Talk about the process or instinct to move these poems (or your work in general) as independent entities into a body of work.

How and why did this happen? Have you had this intention for a while? What encouraged and/or confounded this (or a book, in general) coming together? Was it a struggle?

I struggled with organizing the book into discrete sections. I could think of many different ways the poems might go together. Creating an index of symbols as a tagging system helped me develop an internal order and navigation. Of course, readers are free to engage with the index and symbols as they wish—as hyperlinks, as an alternative language, as game pieces. For me, this mapping was a way to think about how categorization systems create language in somewhat arbitrary and idiosyncratic ways.

This organization allowed me to think of the book as a series of overlapping clouds, and came out of conversations with Afrofuturist playwright Derek McPhatter about clouds and digital archives. This led me to Tung-Hui Hu's book, *A Prehistory of the Cloud*. Hu speaks about the Cloud as an early metaphor of the internet, "a topography or architecture of our own desire," and a space where old and new media are layered on top of each other. The Cloud is a networked, amorphous, decentered space for our online activities, archives, and ghostly footprints. It also refers to our borderless cyber apparatus with workers in Asia and other countries writing code, answering calls, and operating servers that form our networked communications and information systems. Rather than being clean and streamlined, this system is messy with a constant need for updates and fixes. I also played with different literary registers of clouds, as a type of deus ex machina—a god generator in myths and epics. I kept coming back to Wordsworth's "Daffodils" ("I wandered lonely as a cloud."), where a cloud is a lyric search engine in a poem that was part of the colonial education of my parents' generation in India. I started thinking about clouds as a messy, layered type of diasporic identity, expanding and dissipating. In *Imagining Otherwise: Asian American Critique*, Candace Chu discusses the Asian American identity formation as "fantasy links between body and subjectivity discursively forged in legal and literary texts," which I took as a type of cloud identity that is always in process, never fixed.

Did you envision this collection as a collection or understand your process as writing or making specifically around a theme while the poems themselves were being written / the work was being made? How or how not?

Initially, I started this collection with as an ongoing investigation of "avatars." Avatar is the Sanskrit word for descent, and within Hindu cosmology an avatar is the incarnation of a god in material form in times of crisis. It is also the Western word for digital identity or alternative persona. In both cases, avatars imply the possibility of multiple iterations of the self, a type of cloud identity. When I wrote my last book, *The Trouble with Humpadori*, I played with the literal definition of avatar, as descent: specifically, as a descent into an abject body. Humpadori or Hump is a race monster, shifting in and out of multiple iterations of the racialized body in crisis, and morphing into gendered commodity forms. In Daughter Isotope, I play on the digital register of the word avatar, as an uploaded ascent into a floaty cloud realm—where the desire for upgrades follows narratives of assimilation, the search engine, the virus aspiring toward A.I. consciousness, crowdsourced Emily Dickinsons, and various cyber lives. I wander into sacred texts such as the epic Mahabharata, as well digital gaming, the internet, and *The Wizard of Oz*. Krishna, an avatar of the Hindu god Vishnu, is one of the main characters in the Mahabharata, but is also a character in comics and video games. The Mahabharata, an epic about a civil war, is itself a cloud text—with encyclopedic tendencies—and was compiled over centuries. Vyasa, the purported author, whose name means compiler, is a surrogate for the generations of people (gurus and everyday folks like my parents) that created and continue to craft multiple iterations of the epic, which has no absolute definite version, and continues to be reimagined in soap operas, video games, and bedtime stories (my own first encounter).

Famous are these lines from the Mahabharata: "Whatever is here about dharma, profit, pleasure, and release is found elsewhere, but whatever is not here is nowhere else" (translated by Wendy Doniger). These categories of dharma, profit, pleasure, and release determined an ethos of an entire ancient Brahmin world, hierarchical, systematized, and patriarchal. Such taxonomic systems can evoke nostalgia and dangerous nationalistic longings. But I am interested in that nowhere else—the place of the uncategorizable, a site with no fixed location (an @), where I am an unmoored daughter.

What formal structures or other constrictive practices (if any) do you use in the creation of your work? Have certain teachers or instructive environments, or readings/writings/work of other creative people informed the way you work/write?

The structure of video games and gaming worlds really influenced me. The poems in the book started out as my rendering of a multiplayer online game. I created an elaborate system of gameplay/tiers/backstory, which I eventually abandoned. I am also informed by the worldbuilding in the science fiction of Nnedi Okorafor and Nalo Hopkinson, writers who apply cultural mythologies from Nigeria and the Caribbean, respectively, into technological fantasy-scapes.

I think of myself engaging in the aesthetics of the variety show. This formal variety speaks to features of what Arjun Appadurai calls "high globalization," traditional "vertebrate" formal structures that coexist with metastasizing "cellular" infrastructures of our digital networks and affiliations.

Some of the ideas and works that have influenced this book include: Ngũgĩ wa Thiong'o's globalectics and cyberorality, Kamau Brathwaite's video poems, Terrence Hayes anagrammatic procedures, Bollywood storytelling, Arun Kolatkar's *Sarpa Satra*, and Adrienne Rich's *Diving into the Wreck*, Dante's tercets in *The Divine Comedy*, Satyajit Ray's film *Devi*, and poet Monica Mody's feminist critique of Brahmanical Hinduism in her dissertation, "Claiming Voice, Vitality, and Authority in Post-Secular South Asian Borderlands: A Critical Hermeneutics and Autohistoria/Teoría for Decolonial Feminist Consciousness."

Some of the poems came out of collaborations with visual artists (Bishakh Som, Kathy High, and Rachel Simmons). I also worked with choreographer/dancer Daiane Lopes de Silva and choreographer/physicist Weidong Yang, whose *A.I. Sensorium* creates a cyber-imaginary in dance. I began to think of certain poems as dance formations and shaped them accordingly.

Speaking of monikers, what does your title represent? How was it generated? Talk about the way you titled the book, and how your process of naming (individual pieces, sections, etc) influences you and/or colors your work specifically.

When I was a teenager, my dad, who was a civil engineer in the nuclear industry, actually wanted us to collaborate on a screenplay of the Mahabharata in English, a sort of pipedream he had about making movies, despite his more practical profession. At the time, I rolled my eyes. But what happens when a daughter gets hold of the familial/cultural archive? How does it destabilize that archive? The title, "Daughter Isotope," derives from the scientific nomenclature for radioactive decay, in which a parent isotope decays into daughter particles, both stable and unstable. This decay process is used as a form of measurement that determines age across large timescales, but is also harnessed as energy within the atomic industry via a controlled chain reaction. While the first section, "Vyasa Cloud," opens with the Mahabharata, the later sections move into other cosmologies and mythologies in U.S popular culture and media. As the book proceeds, "daughter" genders (such as Draupadi and Emily Dickinson) destabilize and evolve into different versions or avatars (toxic waste-products, strange hybrids, and cyborgs).

What does this book DO (as much as what it says or contains)?

It does: vortex. It does: choose your own adventure. It does: clouds.

What would be the best possible outcome for this book? What might it do in the world, and how will its presence as an object facilitate your creative role in your community and beyond? What are your hopes for this book, and for your practice?

My hopes are for more collaborations. I like to think that the permeability of poetry allows me to settle, if only briefly, into alternative spaces, however flat, congealed, or uncomfortable to me. In my collaborations with professional graphic artists, choreographers, and sound artists, I like to hear my poems spoken by other voices, remixed and made strange to me. I'm reminded that language, even when I use it, does not originate with me, and is always shifting, moving—plural and salivating.

What does it mean to make books in this time, and what are your thoughts around shifting into digital books/objects and digital access in general?

While I love print books, I am all for accessibility and reach, especially in thinking about archives as moving, changing, and expanding. Digital access feels key.

Let's talk a little bit about the role of poetics and creative community in social and political activism, so present in our daily lives as we face the often sobering, sometimes dangerous realities of the Capitalocene. The publication of these volumes now falls during an ongoing global pandemic, intersecting with the largest collective uprising in US history, with Black Lives Matter, dismantling white supremacy, and abolition at the fore. How does your process, practice, or work reflect these conditions?

As Adrienne Rich writes in "North American Time," "Poetry never stood a chance / of standing outside history." I believe any work is embedded in the politics and conditions of its place and time. The time in which these poems were written saw the mainstreaming of white nationalism in the U.S. and Hindu nationalism in India. These virulent movements are not unrelated, generating exclusionary, anti-Muslim policies, perpetuating anti-Black racism, and justifying violence against minorities. The current fear surrounding the Southern (Mexico/U.S.) border is represented sometimes as the foreigner's unassimilable, undigestible alien body, the body that can never be American enough. A big question for me is: How do we upend patriarchal master narratives that support state-sponsored violence when such narratives are often formative? Stories from the epic *Mahabharata* were told to me as a child as epic adventure tales. *The Wizard of Oz*, which I take as a fantasy of the U.S. frontier, originated as a series of children's books by L. Frank Baum, who advocated exterminating Native Americans. For me, tackling some of the stories was a way of questioning the logic of militarism, perpetual war, and state violence. How do some of these narratives go viral, transmit across time and generations? How can we alter them? Is it possible to imagine other communities and affiliations? The internet, home of our social networks, was developed as part of the military complex. In my work, I attempt to explore the features of cyber-communities and transnational networks operating through unofficial channels that engage in alternative imaginaries, at times resistant and hopeful, at times toxic and violent.

I'd be curious to hear some of your thoughts on the challenges we face in speaking and publishing across lines of race, age, ability, class, privilege, social/cultural background, gender, sexuality (and other identifiers) within the community as well as creating and maintaining safe spaces, vs. the dangers of remaining and producing in isolated "silos" and/or disciplinary and/ or institutional bounds?

Institutional support for innovative work across difference remains elusive. Community is everything. Out of necessity, the crisis of the pandemic has created a greater impetus for virtual communities, collectives, and events, not limited by geographical region. Hopefully, some of this energy around virtual community-building persists and forges new artistic alliances—for myself and others.

ABOUT THE AUTHOR

VIDHU AGGARWAL's poetry and multimedia practices engage with world-building, video, and graphic media, drawing mythic schemas from popular culture, science, and ancient texts. Her poetry book, *The Trouble with Humpadori* (2016), imagines a cosmic mythological space for marginalized transnational subjects. Avatara, a chapbook from Portable @Yo-Yo Labs Press, is situated in a post-apocalyptic gaming world where A.I.'s play at being gods. She has published in the *Boston Review, Black Warrior Review, Aster(ix) Journal, Poemelon,* and *Leonardo,* among other journals. She is currently engaging in a "cloud poetics," as a way of thinking about personal, collective, and digital archives as a collaborate process with comic artists, dancers, and video artists. A Djerassi resident and Kundiman fellow, she teaches at Rollins College.

The Operating System uses the language "print document" to differentiate from the book-object as part of our mission to distinguish the act of documentation-in-book-FORM from the act of publishing as a backwards-facing replication of the book's agentive *role* as it may have appeared the last several centuries of its history. Ultimately, I approach the book as TECHNOLOGY: one of a variety of printed documents (in this case, bound) that humans have invented and in turn used to archive and disseminate ideas, beliefs, stories, and other evidence of production.

Ownership and use of printing presses and access to (or restriction of printed materials) has long been a site of struggle, related in many ways to revolutionary activity and the fight for civil rights and free speech all over the world. While (in many countries) the contemporary quotidian landscape has indeed drastically shifted in its access to platforms for sharing information and in the widespread ability to "publish" digitally, even with extremely limited resources, the importance of publication on physical media has not diminished. In fact, this may be the most critical time in recent history for activist groups, artists, and others to insist upon learning, establishing, and encouraging personal and community documentation practices. Hear me out.

With The OS's print endeavors I wanted to open up a conversation about this: the ultimately radical, transgressive act of creating PRINT /DOCUMENTATION in the digital age. It's a question of the archive, and of history: who gets to tell the story, and what evidence of our life, our behaviors, our experiences are we leaving behind? We can know little to nothing about the future into which we're leaving an unprecedentedly digital document trail — but we can be assured that publications, government agencies, museums, schools, and other institutional powers that be will continue to leave BOTH a digital and print version of their production for the official record. Will we?

As a (rogue) anthropologist and long time academic, I can easily pull up many accounts about how lives, behaviors, experiences — how THE STORY of a time or place — was pieced together using the deep study of correspondence, notebooks, and other physical documents which are no longer the norm in many lives and practices. As we move our creative behaviors towards digital note taking, and even audio and video, what can we predict about future technology that is in any way assuring that our stories will be accurately told – or told at all? How will we leave these things for the record? In these documents we say:

WE WERE HERE, WE EXISTED, WE HAVE A DIFFERENT STORY

- *Elæ Moss, Founder/Creative Director*

2020-21

Institution is a Verb: A Panoply Performance Lab Compilation - Esther Neff, Ayana Evans, Tsedaye Makonnen and Elizabeth Lamb, editors.
Vidhu Aggarwal - Daughter Isotope
Johnny Damm - Failure Biographies
Power ON - Ginger Ko
Spite - Danielle Pafunda
Acid Western - Robert Balun

KIN(D)* TEXTS AND PROJECTS

Intergalactic Travels: Poems from a Fugutive Alien - Alan Pelaez Lopez
HOAX - Joey De Jesus [Kin(d)*]
RoseSunWater - Angel Dominguez [Kin(d)*/Glossarium]
Bodies of Work - Elæ Moss & Georgia Elrod

GLOSSARIUM: UNSILENCED TEXTS AND TRANSLATIONS

Steven Alvarez - Manhatitlán [Glossarium]
Híkurí (Peyote) - José Vincente Anaya (tr. Joshua Pollock)
Ernst Toller's "Vormorgen" & Emmy Hennings - Radical Archival Translations - Mathilda Cullen [Glossarium x Kin(d)*; German-English]
Black and Blue Partition ('Mistry) - Monchoachi (tr. Patricia Hartland) [Glossarium; French & Antillean Creole/English]

IN CORPORE SANO

Hypermobilities - Ellen Samuels
Goodbye Wolf-Nik DeDominic

2019

Ark Hive-Marthe Reed
I Made for You a New Machine and All it Does is Hope - Richard Lucyshyn
Illusory Borders-Heidi Reszies
A Year of Misreading the Wildcats - Orchid Tierney
Of Color: Poets' Ways of Making | An Anthology of Essays on Transformative Poetics - Amanda
Galvan Huynh & Luisa A. Igloria, Editors

KIN(D)* TEXTS AND PROJECTS

A Bony Framework for the Tangible Universe-D. Allen [In Corpore Sano]
Opera on TV-James Brunton
Hall of Waters-Berry Grass
Transitional Object-Adrian Silbernagel

GLOSSARIUM: UNSILENCED TEXTS AND TRANSLATIONS

Śnienie / Dreaming - Marta Zelwan/Krystyna Sakowicz,
(Poland, trans. Victoria Miluch)
High Tide Of The Eyes - Bijan Elahi (Farsi-English/dual-language)
trans. Rebecca Ruth Gould and Kayvan Tahmasebian
In the Drying Shed of Souls: Poetry from Cuba's Generation Zero
Katherine Hedeen and Víctor Rodríguez Núñez, translators/editors
Street Gloss - Brent Armendinger with translations of Alejandro Méndez, Mercedes Roffé, Fabián
Casas, Diana Bellessi
& Néstor Perlongher (Argentina)
Operation on a Malignant Body - Sergio Loo
(Mexico, trans. Will Stockton)[In Corpore Sano]
Are There Copper Pipes in Heaven - Katrin Ottarsdóttir
(Faroe Islands, trans. Matthew Landrum)

DOCUMENT

/däkyəmənt/
First meant "instruction" or "evidence," whether written or not.

noun - a piece of written, printed, or electronic matter that provides information or evidence or that serves as an official record *verb* - record (something) in written, photographic, or other form *synonyms* - paper - deed - record - writing - act - instrument

[*Middle English, precept, from Old French, from Latin documentum, example, proof, from docre, to teach; see dek- in Indo-European roots.*]

Who is responsible for the manufacture of value?

Based on what supercilious ontology have we landed in a space where we vie against other creative people in vain pursuit of the fleeting credibilities of the scarcity economy, rather than freely collaborating and sharing openly with each other in ecstatic celebration of MAKING?

While we understand and acknowledge the economic pressures and fear-mongering that threatens to dominate and crush the creative impulse,
we also believe that
now more than ever we have the tools to redistribute agency via cooperative means,
fueled by the fires of the Open Source Movement.

**Looking out across the invisible vistas of that rhizomatic parallel country
we can begin to see our community beyond constraints, in the place where
intention meets resilient, proactive, collaborative organization.**

Here is a document born of that belief, sown purely of imagination and will.
When we document we assert. We print to make real, to reify our being there.
When we do so with mindful intention to address our process, to open our work
to others, to create beauty in words in space, to respect and acknowledge the strength
of the page we now hold physical, a thing in our hand, we remind ourselves that,
like Dorothy: *we had the power all along, my dears.*

the PRINT! DOCUMENT SERIES

is a project of
the trouble with bartleby
in collaboration with
the operating system

CPSIA information can be obtained
at www.ICGtesting.com
Printed in the USA
LVHW011953090921
697444LV00017B/1515

9 781946 031907